D. AND BUCKETS

Resources for a Fuller Life

In His fullness,
Jude 2

by
Calvin S. Metcalf

Calvin S Metcalf

Printed in the United States of America by Publishing and Printing, Inc., Knoxville, Tennessee.

ISBN # 0-89826-078-7

Drawings by Hollie Wohlwend

Extensive effort has been made to credit the sources of copyrighted material used in this book. If any such acknowledgment has been inadvertently omitted or miscredited, receipt of such information would be appreciated.

Some scriptures taken from the HOLY BIBLE, NEW INTERNATIONAL VERSION. Copyright © 1973, 1978, 1984 International Bible Society. Used by permission of Zondervan Bible Publishers.

Some scripture references taken from the following translations:
King James Version
New King James Version
New American Standard Bible

*Lovingly dedicated
to my three grandchildren:*

*Jonathan Stewart Metcalf
Kayla Joy Metcalf*

Haley Marie Olive

ACKNOWLEDGMENTS

My sermons and thoughts are gleaned from a variety of reading sources. I am indebted to such publications as *Preaching*, *Homiletics*, and *Proclaim*, as well as sermon pamphlets by John Claypool and John Killinger. The writings of Charles Swindoll, Max Lucado, Carlyle Marney, J. Wallace Hamilton, Helmut Thielicke, Elton Trueblood, Fred Craddock, and William Willimon have influenced my thought patterns.

I am deeply grateful to my wife Bobbie, who evaluates my sermons and writings and gives me a reader's/listener's perspective. I also acknowledge the contributions of the congregation of Central Baptist Church of Fountain City, Knoxville, Tennessee. They have challenged me for almost twenty-two years to do my best in preaching and writing. It has been a fellowship of studying, thinking, and praying as together we have searched for truth.

TABLE OF CONTENTS

PREFACE

In the movie *Shadowlands*, C. S. Lewis makes the following statement to his class: "We read to let ourselves know we are not alone." Reading books and writing books are processes of communication. We connect with a larger fellowship of learners as we read and as we write. What a lonely world it would be if we had nothing to read and no one to whom we could write! From the Christian perspective, we are admonished to study and show ourselves approved unto God, workers who need not be ashamed of our credentials.

As readers, we never learn it all, and as writers, we never say it all. Writing a book, in one sense, is a bit presumptuous. The writer is suggesting that he or she has something to say, and there are folks eager to read it. In writing as well as in reading, we gain most from understanding that we are learners. No one can be taught who has not first known the humility of his or her own ignorance. A lazy mind will often disguise shallowness with meaningless verbiage. Often the lack of learning heralds itself as an authority on every subject. Our hope is to follow truth wherever it leads, rather than try to lead truth down the path of our own opinions.

Dippers and Buckets is a book designed to get something going between the reader and God. Hopefully, you will find learning as well as fellowship in these pages. Included are sermons, punctuated by appropriate reflections and prayers. This format focuses our attention on preaching, thinking, and praying as ways of learning and doing the Christian faith.

Dippers and Buckets deals with bits and pieces of gospel truth. There is no presumption that this is the final word on anything. I am fully aware that we learn and grow by our daily exposure to the thoughts and ideas of others who struggle to know God in a healthy context. My freedom for sharing the thoughts of this book comes from not having to know everything, but learning to trust God Who does.

Appreciation is expressed to Robin Rosser for her typing, editing, and general consultation in the formation of this book.

Chapter 1

DIPPERS AND BUCKETS

II Corinthians 2:5-11; Galatians 6:1-5;

Ephesians 4:29-32

Although the title "Dippers and Buckets"* may sound a bit strange, it symbolizes two of the most basic aspects of our human personalities. We all have dippers and we all have buckets. The way in which we use each of these will determine our quality of life.

Let me define what I mean by each of these symbols. *Buckets* represents that resource of emotional and spiritual sustenance from which we draw to live our daily lives. It is that sense of self-worth and godly well-being. It's what Jesus meant when He said, "I have come that you might have life and have it more abundantly." He might well have said, "I have come that you might have a full bucket."

My use of *bucket* is the same as in the song which says, "Fill my cup, Lord . . . fill it up and make me whole." Sometimes we live out of the context of an overflowing bucket, and life is wholesome and abundant. But then again, we live out of an empty bucket, and life is complicated and painful.

*The idea for "Dippers and Buckets" came from an unknown source shared in a handout from the Baptist Sunday School Board in 1987 by William E. "Bill" Young.

9

There are many things that can fill our buckets. For example, suppose you went to church and somebody said, "Good morning." Now that would fill your bucket a little because someone was aware of your existence. We live in a desert of unawareness where people every day pass us by without even recognizing we are alive.

But what if instead of just saying "Good morning," someone said, "Good morning, John," or Joe or Mary or Linda or whoever. Now that would fill your bucket a little more, because you have a name and you are a person. We all need to be recognized, not just as a person but as some special person with a name.

Let's go one step further and say someone said as they greeted you, "I've been praying for you," or, "How is your family?" That would fill your bucket a lot because someone knew about your circumstances and expressed care for you. It fills your bucket to know that others understand and care.

There are many other things which fill our buckets. Have you ever had a day in which you felt your bucket was so full you could face almost anything? The toughest problems are much easier to deal with when your bucket is full.

The flip side of this matter is that we also have *dippers*, and we tend to get our dippers in each other's buckets. For example, suppose you got to church on time, but as you were getting out of your car, you tore your skirt and had to return home to change.

Frustrated and embarrassed, you came in as inconspicuously as possible. But someone made a big deal about your being late. That someone got his dipper in your bucket.

Let's say you're at a banquet--a very special banquet with pretty tablecloths--and you knock over your coffee, staining the white lace as it runs across the table. You are quite embarrassed and want to find a place to crawl off and hide. Most of the people are understanding and kind. But ol' Bright Eyes down the table shouts so that almost everybody can hear, "Hey! You spilled your coffee!" He got his dipper in your bucket.

Your son comes in with a report card of which he is fairly proud. You say to him loudly, "You only got one 'A'?" You got your great big dipper in his little bucket.

There are a lot of dippers out there trying to get into our buckets. If we're not careful we'll let our buckets get empty. And have you ever noticed that when your bucket is empty is when you are the most irritable? You chase people away when you need them the most. We become obnoxious when our buckets are empty, and we go around with our dippers out. We keep trying to get our dippers in other people's buckets, and they do not like it.

There is a trap here. Have you ever noticed how good it feels to get your dipper in someone's bucket by pointing out their mistakes? We seem to take some kind of morbid delight in verbally punishing those who

11

have violated our code of behavior. We can't seem to wait to tell folks they forgot, or messed up the program, or disappointed us. It feels like we are filling our buckets from theirs, but in reality we are taking from both.

Some years ago a lady came to me to complain about an incident, and then said with a great deal of relief, "Well, I'm glad I got that off my chest!" Perhaps she felt a lot better, but I felt like a heel. She got her dipper in my bucket.

We can't fill our buckets by dipping out of someone else's bucket. The only way to fill our own buckets is to help fill someone else's bucket. The gospel of grace is our best resource for getting all our buckets full.

Now let us turn to our scripture. Following are three passages which deal with this matter of dippers and buckets. The first passage is II Corinthians 2:5-11:

> If anyone has caused grief, he has not so much grieved me as he has grieved all of you, to some extent--not to put it too severely. The punishment inflicted on him by the majority is sufficient for him. Now instead, you ought to forgive and comfort him, so that he will not be overwhelmed by excessive sorrow. I urge you, therefore, to reaffirm your love for him. The reason I wrote you was to see if you would stand the

test and be obedient in everything. If
you forgive anyone, I also forgive him.
And what I have forgiven--if there was
anything to forgive--I have forgiven in
the sight of Christ for your sake, in order
that Satan might not outwit us. For we
are not unaware of his schemes.

In this passage Paul appeals for forgiveness
toward a person who had offended him, as well as the
church at Corinth. Paul felt the person in question had
been sufficiently disciplined. He wanted the church to
affirm its love toward him and stop dipping out of his
bucket. He wanted restoration and grace to fill up the
offender's bucket so that Satan would not use the
episode for his evil purposes and perhaps cause further
confusion in the church. People with empty buckets
cause havoc in the church, and Paul knew this.

The second passage is Galatians 6:1-5:

Brothers, if someone is caught in
a sin, you who are spiritual should restore
him gently. But watch yourself, or you
also may be tempted. Carry each other's
burdens, and in this way you will fulfill
the law of Christ. If anyone thinks he is
something when he is nothing, he
deceives himself. Each one should test
his own actions. Then he can take pride
in himself, without comparing himself to

somebody else, for each one should carry his own load.

In this passage Paul emphasizes the healing fellowship of the church. He accented the fact that church people must lean on one another. They must not be judgmental, pointing out each other's faults, dipping out of each other's buckets. Paul writes that the real law of Christ instructs them to *bear* one another's burdens, and so fill up one another's buckets. Galatian Christians had let their buckets get empty, and they had become terribly legalistic. They needed love and nurture; they needed a whole bucketful of grace.

The third passage is Ephesians 4:29-32:

> Do not let any unwholesome talk come out of your mouths, but only what is helpful for building others up according to their needs, that it may benefit those who listen. And do not grieve the Holy Spirit of God, with whom you were sealed for the day of redemption. Get rid of all bitterness, rage and anger, brawling and slander, along with every form of malice. Be kind and compassionate to one another, forgiving each other, just as in Christ God forgave you.

Paul wanted the Christians of Ephesus to talk kindly *about* one another and *to* one another. Apparently they had grieved the Holy Spirit by their godless conversations about one another. Paul wanted all bitterness and anger and evil speaking to be done with. His appeal was for forgiveness, to forget things even as Christ forgave and forgot. We get our dippers in each other's buckets more by what we say than any other way.

With these verses of scripture as a background, let's look at some ways in which we can help fill one another's buckets.

In the first place, we can develop a godly compassion. Paul encourages us as well as early Christians to learn from the gentle nature of Jesus how to relate to one another. Our Lord's attitude was one of kindness and courtesy. His compassion in every sinful circumstance is a pattern for us to follow. We can learn from our Lord a sense of deep appreciation for people which causes us to be more kind and considerate.

Often we are much too volatile and vocal in the expression of our opinions. It seems that anger and not anguish is the prevailing emotion when disagreement occurs. Even in church we become harsh and critical toward those who see life from another perspective. We tend to verbally assassinate those who would dare disagree with us. It would be better to flavor our convictions with courtesy and to control our competitive spirits with compassion.

15

Where in the world did we ever get the idea we could win the world by forcing our own opinions upon it? Jesus made it clear: "Unless a grain of wheat is planted and dies, it does not produce." We have a lot to learn about dying. If only we could see the quiet possibilities in the calm and courageous disposition of our Lord, we would never again need to be argumentative about our faith.

The truth of God about which we witness comes in a container of kindness or else it loses its appeal. Love is never promoted in a hateful way. Our Lord still yearns for us to turn the other cheek and go the second mile. In kindness and compassion we put a lot of fullness in other people's buckets.

In the second place, if we want to stop dipping out of each other's buckets, then we must learn to forgive. *Forgiveness* was Paul's watchword in dealing with every awkward situation which the churches faced. It was vital then and it is vital now to the development of good personal relationships. Our Lord taught the value of forgiveness by both word and deed.

How well do you forgive? Do you enjoy harboring grudges against those who have mistreated you? Forgiveness will elude you if you delight in reciting your stories of oppression. In your own mind the offense will grow bigger every time you tell it. In fact, it will soon outgrow the truth so that you who are offended will soon become an offender by your exaggeration.

An unforgiving spirit is a terrible temperament.

16

It reaches out a hand of hostility toward anyone who does not sympathize with its belligerence. The fellowship of resentment is a miserable group because the sessions always focus on the negative. Joy and praise are eliminated by an awkward need to verbally chastise one another.

I likewise ask not only "How well do you forgive?" but "How well do you forget?" Are you a "rememberer" or a "reconciler"? If you have a capacity to lose the memory of wrong in the joy of reconciliation, forgiveness will be your sweet reward. The burden of revenge is a heavy load to carry. The need to retaliate is a demanding routine that can and must be eliminated.

Unload your burdened soul and find rest in the Lord. Go to someone with whom you have had a misunderstanding and display a spirit of reconciliation. Go out of your way to be nice to someone who may not have been nice to you. Pray for people with whom you disagree. Ask God to give them joy and peace. When this is done, you will fill not only their buckets, but you will add a lot to your own.

In the third place, if we want to stop dipping out of other people's buckets then we must learn the value of pleasant speech. The ability to speak kindly on any issue is a gift of grace. A pleasing attitude is the product of a godly disposition. A close relationship with Christ is always evident in what we say and how we say it. Conversation that is uplifting and helpful emerges from deeper conversation with our living Lord.

Whatever joy we have in Christ finds expression in the way we talk to one another and the way we talk about one another. To have our own sins forgiven is to converse redemptively about the sins of others. To sense the heart of God's love for all humanity is a prerequisite for compassionate speech. To grasp our Lord's positive approach to the future is to have a flavor of hope in everything we say. Pleasant words are valuable to the kind of witness we bear for our Lord.

On the other hand, negative and critical conversation is evidence of a hostile spirit. To hear some people talk, you wonder at whom are they mad? With whom are they trying to get even? Sometimes bitterness emerges when there are sins and burdens we have not taken to the Lord. An unwillingness to forgive and an unwillingness to be forgiven often create words of an unpleasant nature. No one enjoys a bitter person because the conversation is always depressing.

There is an awesome sadness about folk who have lost hope, and their words express that despair. Therefore, let us monitor our own speech and determine if we are bearing witness to the bad news of man or to the good news of God. After all, our Lord reminds us that by our words we shall be justified, and by our words we shall be condemned.

Do you have the gift of pleasant words? The writer of Proverbs says, "A gentle answer turns away wrath, but a harsh word stirs up anger. The tongue that brings healing is a tree of life, but a deceitful tongue crushes the spirit."

Do you want to see a miracle? Then plant a word of love heart-deep in a person's life. Nurture it with a smile and with a prayer, and then watch his or her bucket fill up.

You see, with our words we have the ability to either curse or bless another person. With our words of cursing we tend to be negative, nagging, and critical, and in so doing, we get our dippers in their buckets. With our words of blessing, however, we share our energy, our praise, and our prayers, and in so doing, we fill up someone else's bucket.

The conclusion of this matter is rather simple. We can start building up one another. We can stop dipping out of each other's buckets. This can be accomplished by a godly compassion, by forgiveness, and by pleasant speech. I think we know how to do it --it's just that our own buckets are so empty. We find ourselves with little thought trying to dip out of one another's buckets. Let's hear Paul well when he writes about "bearing one another's burdens," "being kind and tenderhearted," and "forgiving one another as Christ has forgiven us."

One of the highlights of the spiritual growth program called *MasterLife* is what is referred to as a "strength rally." It is a time when participants go around the circle of eight or ten people involved, and each person is reminded of his or her strengths. Nothing negative is stated; only encouraging and positive and complimentary remarks are made to each person.

Now that's what church ought to be. It ought to be a strength rally. That's what family ought to be--a strength rally. That's what Christian witness is all about--going forth to build people up, to fill their buckets, not to go dipping into other people's buckets.

If you need a fuller bucket, if you *want* a fuller bucket, it can begin at some altar, where you receive Christ as your Savior, recommit your life to Him, and join a fellowship of bucket-fillers.

Fred Craddock's poet friend leaves us with a fitting thought:

> Lying thinking last night
> how to find my soul a home,
> where water is not thirsty
> and loaf bread is not stone.
> I came up with one thing,
> and I think I'm not wrong.
> No one, but no one,
> can make it all alone.

20

REFLECTION

Someone has said of a certain church member, "She makes me feel as if I have had a bath in sunshine." What a beautiful way to describe someone who has such an uplifting effect on others! Surely this was the plan of Jesus as He taught us to find beauty and to create beauty in the way we live. While on earth He gave everyone He encountered a bath in sunshine. He encouraged folk whose lives, for the most part, had bottomed out. Instead of rejecting them He wanted them to have another chance. His attitude was one of compassion rather than condemnation, cleansing rather than criticizing, healing rather than hurt, and love rather than hate.

Jesus began His Sermon on the Mount with what we call "the Beatitudes." These are "happiness" words. He gave His listeners a lesson in joy. He taught them how to bathe themselves in the sunshine of God's love and then go forth to share goodwill with others. Jesus wanted people to be happy because He knew happy people are most likely to be good people.

The people with whom Jesus had the most difficulty were folk who hindered happiness. Legalistic people who make religion a load instead of a lift were the topic of our Lord's strongest words of rebuke. Jesus could not tolerate a faith that had no joy or a commitment that had no love. He disliked the attitudes and actions of religious leaders who spread more gloom than gladness.

Peddlers of sadness will always do more harm than good no matter how noteworthy their causes. People who "ugly up" happiness for others will never bathe anyone in sunshine. Busybody Christians will never become saints. They are too busy tearing others down in order to make themselves look good. True saints are never aware of their sainthood. They have an unassuming fragrance and beauty which make them sunshine people.

Only God can make us this way. He who has the power to get us to heaven has the ability to give us some heaven here. Likewise, He who has the power to keep us out of hell can take some hell out of our lives here. He can take the water of our despair and turn it into the wine of our joy. He is a God of gladness who can put sunshine into our souls, singing in our voices, optimism in our attitudes, and heaven in our future.

PRAYER

Thank You, Lord, for the abundant life.
Thank You for giving us divine resources
to help us live within the context of Your will.
We are grateful for people who contribute
to our emotional and spiritual fullness.
They love us and encourage us
along the journey.
At times, O Lord, our cups run over
as goodness and mercy follow us
on our pilgrimage of life.
We draw from the wells
of spiritual refreshment.
We bask in the sunlight of Your love.
We feast on Your heavenly manna.
We are, indeed, recipients of grace.
But our lives, O Lord,
are not always lived with a full bucket.
People near and dear to us
dip from our precious resources.
We allow circumstances to deplete us.
We lose our fullness
by giving out more than we take in.
Revenge has robbed us of a forgiving spirit.
Bitterness has taken its toll on our compassion.
Despair has drained our cup of joy.
We cry out to You, O Lord,
and ask that You refuel the fire of our enthusiasm.
Quicken us by Your Holy Spirit.

Fill the emptiness of our lives
with the fullness of Your hope.
Help us plug the holes in our leaking buckets
so that we may bless others
with our fullness.
Amen.

Chapter 2

EDEN CLOSED--KINGDOM OPEN

Genesis 1:27-28, 2:8-9, 3:22-24; Matthew 6:10

We know very little about the garden of Eden. Our best resource is Genesis. What we *do* know leads us to believe the garden of Eden represents the ultimate in terms of human happiness, divine fulfillment, and creative possibility. In that state of innocence, Adam and Eve had perfect harmony with God and nature. During the tender time of creation's beginning, God found great pleasure in that which He had made. Everything our minds can imagine in terms of perfection, peace, and divine presence is symbolized by the garden of Eden.

But it did not last. Adam and Eve sinned away the right to live in that eternal bliss. They lost the paradise of God by willful disobedience. Their sin prompted their expulsion from the garden with penalties and limitations which culminated in eventual physical death. The Fall was a sadness for the whole human race. Because of the Fall, we all have become afflicted with an ailment from which we have not survived. That ailment is sin.

Here we are, thousands and thousands of years later, still adjusting to the fact that Eden is closed. We are still searching for it. We are frantically looking for some utopia. We search diligently for some perfect place where sin and pain will not find us. The tragedy is that sin has a way of destroying any Eden we may think we have discovered. Evil tears down the possibility of any utopia we seek to construct. The awesome reality is that we live in a fallen world. Sin has taken its toll on Mother Earth and her inhabitants.

We need not lose ourselves, however, in hopeless despair, because our loving God has interjected grace. Although Eden is closed, the kingdom is open. God has another way. The history of sin is superseded only by the history of grace. As Paul expressed it in Romans 5:19-20, "For as by one man's disobedience many were made sinners, so by the obedience of one shall many be made righteous. Where sin abounded, grace did much more abound." Yes, Eden is closed. The sin of man made it so. But the righteousness of one man, Christ Jesus, has opened a kingdom, and whosoever will may come.

Here, then, is the pivotal truth for any witness, ministry, or mission in which we may engage. Eden is closed. Chaos abounds. Sin is rampant. Disease prevails. But the kingdom is open! The bad news of the human race is that God's original plan was thwarted by sin.

But the good news is God was not taken by surprise. The Bible does not picture God hurrying around through time, trying to meet an unexpected emergency. No sooner had sin entered the garden than God spoke of One who would bruise the serpent's head, and His own heel would be bruised in the process. "In the beginning was the Word," writes John. "The Lamb was slain from the foundation of the world," cries Revelation 13:8. No, no, God was not caught off guard. Even though His disobedient creatures closed down Eden, His kingdom can come and His will can be done on earth, even as it is in heaven.

What does this mean for us in this fellowship of grace? What truth emerges for us who struggle to share this bit of the kingdom together in Christ Jesus?

For one thing, because Eden is closed, we live in a world of hurt and hate. Yet the kingdom is open to offer healing love. The real world in which we live is one of pain. We are called into the kind of life as Christians and as sinners in which we can be hurt. None of us is exempt from the tragedy and chaos of life. Sooner or later we all face the trauma of life's consequences.

In the comic strip "Peanuts," Snoopy is shown on his doghouse typing a novel. He begins his story as always with the words "It was a dark and stormy night." Lucy happens by and, reading over his shoulders, begins to scold the dog unmercifully. "You stupid dog! That's the dumbest thing I ever read! Don't you know that good stories begin 'Once upon a time'?" She leaves, saying, "Dumb, dumb, dumb dog." The last frame of the comic strip shows Snoopy starting his story all over. This time he types, "Once upon a time, it was a dark and stormy night."

Because Eden is closed, we all live in a dark and

stormy world which has a capacity for hurt and hate for each of us. Tragedy strikes. Death is imminent. Character assassins are ready to spread their venom. Temptation is overwhelming. Violence and crime complicate our lives. Wars and rumors of war prevail. Sin abounds. Eden is closed!

It is tough living outside Eden because we never know when we will be the next victim of life's harsh actualities. Let us not needlessly despair, however, for the kingdom is open to offer healing love. God in His loving wisdom knows that in one way or another we have all been hurt. We have the scars to prove it.

Have you ever considered scars? They offer us an interesting revelation. For one thing, they remind us that we have been injured. They also indicate that healing has happened. We are free to focus on either of these two facts. If we choose, we can allow our scars to keep our injuries ever before us. We can readily recall all those folk who have caused us pain. We can continually curse the circumstances that have hurt us. If we get angry enough, we can even shake our fists at God for allowing us to have troubled times. Yes, if we wish, scars can be an awful reminder that bad things have happened to us.

On the other hand, however, scars can help us focus on healing rather than hurt. If we choose, we can gratefully remember the process of forgiveness. We can finger lovingly the pages of scripture that brought health to our souls. In love we can humbly rejoice over the growth that came through our painful chastisements. In faith we can place the scars of our past into the nail-scarred hands of Jesus as we celebrate the possibility of future recoveries. Yes, scars can be a sign that healing has happened. Because Eden is closed, we have many injuries and scars, but the kingdom is open to provide healing and restoration.

In the second place, because Eden is closed, we live in a world that is lost and struggling in its sinfulness. Yet the kingdom is open to invite whosoever will to come and drink of the water of life freely. Because Eden is closed, we live in a world of evangelistic opportunity, and the kingdom is open to give us a base of operation.

The cumulative effect of Eden's closure upon our world even today is devastating. Not only have we messed up Eden, but we now have the capacity to destroy the world God has given us. Sin has equipped our world with an awesome ability to rebel against God and sow the terrible seeds of our own destruction. A sense of hopelessness seems to have settled across our world like a depressing fog as we struggle with the consequences of sin.

Although it appears that our planet Earth is terminally ill, the kingdom is open to offer hope. The kingdom is open to remind us that our destination is not a return to Eden but to arrive at new Jerusalem, the city of God, not built with human hands, eternal in the heavens. Our survival belongs to God. Because of Who He is, we can share Christ with courage, confidence, and optimism.

One of the miracles of the kingdom is that God through the ages has equipped His people with a vision for worldwide proclamation. The call still comes ringing for those who are willing to go and willing to give. The combined energies and excitement of every believer are the ingredients for evangelizing the world. Because the kingdom is open, there is no place so distant, no language so difficult, and no people so pagan that a godly witness cannot penetrate. The task of witnessing is not merely a human endeavor. Its call comes from the heart of God. Its motivation comes from the will of God. And its accomplishment comes from the power of God. In no way are we nearer the heartbeat of God than when we join His task force for telling the good news. The real answer to the problems of our world is not force, but faith. Not hate, but love. Not greed, but grace. Not revenge, but forgiveness. What a joy to join the Father in the salvation of His children! The kingdom is open to give us a reason to witness and a place for everyone to begin again.

In the third place, because Eden is closed, we live in a divided world, but the kingdom is open to provide a setting for togetherness.

We live in a world of complicated diversity. For some reason, God did not choose to create us all alike. The awesome problems of our world often arise from the fact that we have not learned to deal with these sometimes devastating differences. People all over the world are divided into competing camps of thought on politics, religion, war, sex, economics, and any number of public and private issues. We are divided by external things such as geography and race and gender and age.

The kingdom is open, however, to give us a love which allows us to celebrate our uniqueness and our diversities. In Christ Jesus we are not called to be identical twins; we are called to be brothers and sisters. From the obvious diversity among us we must assume God intends for us to bloom where we have been planted. He wants us to express the fragrance that is naturally ours. Lest we violate His grace, we must humbly invest our diversity into His unity. In Christ, we blend our individual gifts and our unique personalities into the process of being the people of God.

Have you ever considered the diversity among Jesus' disciples? They represented everything from political activists who hated Rome to tax collectors who had sold their souls to Rome. Yet Jesus molded them into a fellowship of love. He inspired unity in the midst of their diversity.

Jesus established His kingdom in order to deal with a divided world. In many ways He has provided for our oneness of spirit and purpose. God has given us His holy, inspired Word to be a resource for unity, not a vehicle for debate. God sent His virgin-born Son into the world to be our Savior, not to divide us over how it happened. Jesus performed miracles of healing, signs, and wonders to reveal the almighty God at work, not to create a climate of controversy. He did not die on a cross in excruciating pain that we might entertain ourselves with theories of atonement. Our Lord's resurrection from the dead was to give us hope and to rally us all together around the greatest event in human history.

The Holy Spirit came to give us the energy for unity and not just to focus our attention on tongues and super-emotionalisms. Our Lord has given us spiritual gifts to build up the body, not to compete in religious popularity contests as to who is the greatest in the kingdom. The book of Revelation was given to show us a godly sense of purpose and meaning to the end times. Never once does it invite us to argue about the Second Coming.

The Lord established the church as a setting for togetherness. In it we learn to be brothers and sisters in Christ. Church was never intended to be a pit in which we hiss at one another, feuding over who is closest to the Lord Jesus. The gospel of the kingdom was designed to bring a divided world together around a love that was so obvious it would discourage our argumentative and competitive tendencies. God help us if in our study of God's word we allow the devil to divert us from the content to the container! We will have missed the kingdom altogether if we become religious instead of righteous. Because Eden is closed, we live in a divided world, but the kingdom is open to rally us around our togetherness in the Lordship of Jesus.

The giant redwood trees of California are the

tallest in the world; some reach heights of 300 feet. You would think that such a tree would have a root system that reaches deep into the earth. However, the opposite is true. The redwoods have a fairly shallow root system. But their roots grow together, intermingled with the roots of other trees. As a result, the massive root system of a forest full of trees helps them all survive the wind and storms.

The kingdom is open to provide us this kind of togetherness and to keep us whenever storms prevail. If you and I belong to Christ, we are a part of that massive root system. Our roots are tied together because He that is in us is greater than he that is in the world.

What if the Lord opened our eyes and showed us the full potential of our church? Would our level of commitment embarrass us? Or would it inspire us to help God realize His dream for us? What does God expect from this body of faith? What is before us?

There is always a future tense to the gospel. The unrealized dream is ever before us. The harvest is always anticipated. The kingdom is always coming! God calls us into tomorrow with the force of a mighty conquest. Let us move faithfully and enthusiastically towards God's eternity.

Yes, Eden is closed. Utopia is a myth. But praise God, the kingdom is open! Can you pray, "Thy kingdom come, Thy will be done in my life and on earth as it is in heaven"?

REFLECTION

There is an interesting diversity in my backyard. On any given morning a variety of animals help themselves to whatever it has to offer. A rabbit nibbles on the tender grass near the garden. Two or three squirrels search for nuts they hid last fall. Birds such as robins, blue jays, cardinals, woodpeckers, crows, and an assortment of smaller ones work the trees and the grass. Occasionally a chipmunk will seek sunlight and food before going underground again.

The fascinating thing about my mini-zoo is how well its inhabitants accept one another. The rabbit doesn't mind sharing the yard with squirrels and birds. The birds seem to have no problem that among them are red, blue, brown, and black species. All the animals accept the diversity of that part of their world.

Would that we humans could make a similar adjustment to the beautiful variety that exists among us! There is surely such a place and a plan for each of us in God's economy. His will is that we share the backyards of our lives with whoever is there.

Occasionally the neighbor's cat strolls across my lawn. His presence sends squirrels scurrying up the trees, birds retreating to the highest limbs, rabbits running into the brush, and chipmunks burrowing into their holes. They all run because the cat is an animal of prey. He will not allow them the freedom to roam my yard. In fear they adjust their lifestyles when the cat is around.

Some people are predators also. They do not accept diversity. They want to eat and devour those who are different. They want the backyard to have only their kind of creatures. Some of these folk are religious predators who hate and harm in the name of their god. They send people hurrying to their hiding places in order to escape rigidity and judgmental dispositions.

My backyard is a parable. It reminds me that I live in God's backyard, and He wants me to accept and share His delight in the variety of folk who use it. Perhaps my backyard is teaching me what true religion is all about. I must reach out to all kinds of people and share the love God has graciously given.

PRAYER

Lord God of heaven and earth,
we are impressed by Your willingness
to look in upon us
and nudge us toward righteous living.
We are overwhelmed
by Your invitation
for us to share in Your kingdom enterprise.
We are humbled
by Your desire to save us.
Hear our prayers of confession.
Listen to us, O Lord,
as we seek to repent of all those sins
which keep us from being kingdom people.
Although we have failed,
we do not wish to be failures.
Although we have been distant,
we do not wish to be strangers.
Although we have missed the mark,
keep us on target.
Give us Your kingdom power
so that in Your name
we may have a ministry of love.
Condition us by Your grace
to be more than what we have ever been.
Amen.

Chapter 3

AN OBSESSION WITH JESUS

Matthew 16:21-28

Obsession is sometimes a strange and cruel element of our human personality. It is often seen as a negative characteristic, and well it can be. Obsession can bring out our worst as it allows awkward feelings and impulses to gain control of our thoughts and our behavior. For example, if mistreated we become obsessed with revenge unless we cultivate a forgiving spirit. If misfortune happens, we sometimes become obsessed with self-pity unless we seek to find the meaning of our pain. If prosperity occurs, we become obsessed with our wealth unless we discover the freedom of God's stewardship. If ambition is strong, we can become obsessed with our success unless we learn the secret of self-denial. If temptation is tolerated, we become obsessed with sinful pleasure unless we learn to wear the armor of Christ. Evil has a terrible tendency to become an obsession in our lives if Jesus is not Lord.

The good news about obsession, however, is that it can have a positive as well as a negative connotation. The only way to offset the obsessive power of evil is to become obsessed with the goodness and grace of our Lord Jesus Christ. The word *obsession* means a state of being under the influence of a feeling, an idea, or an impulse that one cannot escape. There is nothing wrong in being captured by a powerful influence if indeed it is good for us.

To be obsessed, therefore, with good is as much a possibility for us as being obsessed with evil. Is this not what it means to be a Christian? Being a Christian means becoming so enamored with Christ that His will becomes our will. His thoughts become our thoughts, and His way becomes our way.

In our scripture, Jesus was calling for a radical commitment from His followers. Some of the words and phrases of Jesus' challenge leap out at us, such as *dying, resurrection, denying oneself, take up the cross,* and *losing life to find it.* These are powerful and extreme words. They lead us to believe that only those who have found in Jesus a magnificent obsession can meet the Lord's requirements.

At Caesarea Philippi that day, Jesus could not accept the protectionism of Simon Peter. When Jesus talked about going back to Jerusalem, suffering, and dying, Simon Peter seriously objected. He wanted Jesus to find an easier way to be Messiah.

There was no easier way for Him to be Messiah, and there is no easier way for us to be His followers. Messiah must suffer. God must make His loving sacrifice. And all of us who share in His redemptive effort will feel the pain.

We see this beautiful obsession with Jesus demonstrated in the lives of those early Christians.

They were captivated by the demands of Jesus. They came under the spell of Christ and were motivated by His Holy Spirit.

For example, when Peter and John were brought before the authorities and commanded not to speak anymore in Jesus' name, they could not comply. Their words were simple but profound. "Is it better to obey God or man?" they asked. "We cannot help but speak about what we have heard and seen." Those early saints were caught up in a magnificent obsession. They had literally lost themselves in something much bigger than their own safety. In reckless abandon they sold everything and gave everything.

The apostle Paul was captured by this magnificent obsession. He summarized his obsession with the phrase "to live is Christ and to die is gain." He went from persecution to persecution establishing churches and encouraging believers to "be strong in the Lord."

Peter shouted from his epistle, "To God be the glory, both now and forever." The book of Revelation highlights this obsession when it says, "The Lord God omnipotent reigneth forever and ever."

But where are we today? Where are we who claim to be the twentieth-century protectors of this flame? Will we huddle over this flickering fire until we all but smother the light of God? Will we step back and let the fire of heaven consume our carnal desires? Will we let it burn in our bosoms with a word of hope for a cold, callous church and our lost, dying world?

We too must be magnificently obsessed by our Lord Christ. We must not sound an uncertain note. We must not seek an easier way. We must not greatly reduce our Lord's appeal upon our world.

In many ways, as far as the church is concerned, this obsession with Jesus must begin with the pastor and church leaders. There is no way they can escape the biblical mandate to challenge, to inspire, and to prod church members toward greater commitment. In turn, church members are under heavy obligation to accept the awesome assignment of being the people of God. As a body of believers, all must be busy about the things which have captured their hearts' affections and their minds' attention concerning Jesus.

What, then, does it mean to have Jesus as our magnificent obsession? What is the spiritual profile of those whose eyes are fixed on Jesus?

In the first place, people who are beautifully obsessed with Jesus are learning to deal with their sin problem. They have found in Jesus the only way out of the prison of iniquity. They have learned to appropriate I John 1:9, which says, "If we confess our sins, He is faithful and just to forgive us our sins and to cleanse us from all unrighteousness."

This is what makes Jesus so attractive. He does not come to us with bitter vengeance, but with a broken heart. He teaches us to accept His atonement for our sins rather than try to produce our own. No amount of self-inflicted punishment or mental self-ridicule can relieve the anguish of a guilty conscience. Only Jesus has paid the price, and only Jesus can give us the joy of forgiveness.

This does not mean, however, that people who are obsessed with Jesus are less sinful than others. It does mean they have learned to repent, to confess, and to function within the context of grace. They are not defeated by their sins. They have learned from failure to be humble and not bitter. They have learned to be cautious and not arrogant. They have learned to be kind and not condemning.

Furthermore, folk who are learning to deal with the sin problem no longer have to make excuses for their misdeeds. They no longer have to blame others when conflict occurs. They do not have to take out their guilt frustrations on innocent bystanders. Forgiven people have a wholesome and positive attitude toward life. They have nothing to prove except their ability to trust Jesus.

John Newton became an orphan as a young boy. He wandered the streets of London until he learned to navigate a ship. His life as a sailor was rough and rugged. His adventures were as sinful as they were painful. Evil gripped his soul. His drinking got him into serious trouble, and at times it almost cost him his life.

One night after being beaten and thrown into the ship's prison, he turned toward God and gave his heart to Christ. It made a profound difference in him. Not only did he become a successful merchant, he became

41

a writer of hymns. No doubt his most famous is "Amazing Grace, How Sweet the Sound." The ability of God's grace to conquer his sin made Jesus his magnificent obsession. Like John Newton, people obsessed with Jesus are learning to deal with sin.

In the second place, people who are beautifully obsessed with Jesus have a personal relationship with Him. To them, Jesus is not some distant deity who requires occasional attention. He is a daily contributor to their lives.

Here again is a reason why Jesus is so attractive. He is with us, and He is involved. When we pray, He prays with us. When we sing, He joins the celebration. When we worship, He is present. When we hurt, He feels the pain. When we sin, He reprimands. When we succeed, He is pleased. When we die, He holds our hand.

The exciting thing about Jesus is that He comes to us where we are. He meets us in the "everydayness" of life to be our personal friend. The gospels remind us that Jesus did not find His first followers by posting a notice on the temple door. Instead, Jesus went to where they were and to the level of their existence. He went to where they lived their lives and cultivated personal friendships that survived difficulty, danger, and death.

It is true that you and I may find Jesus in some place of worship. We may find Him there as we sing, pray, and worship together. But please remember! Although we meet Him there and find Him there, He insists on going home with us. People for whom Jesus is a magnificent obsession take the name and the person of Jesus with them wherever they go.

As important as it is to know Jesus, it is life-changing to understand that He likewise knows us. A lad of five was being taught to say the Lord's Prayer. He knelt beside his bed one night, and in his first attempt to say it by himself, this is what he said: "Our Father who art in heaven, how do You know my name?" Was he struggling with the big word *hallowed*, or was he saying something more profound than he realized? This is more than a childish struggle to say the right words. God does know our names.

If the Bible teaches anything, it is that our relationship with God is personal. Is not this the impact of Jesus' words when He said, "Not even a sparrow falls apart from the Father's awareness, and even the very hairs of our head are numbered"? We might say with all assurance that God in Jesus Christ has a beautiful obsession with us. To understand this and to feel its impact on our lives is to be caught up in the excitement of living in Christ Jesus.

In the third place, people who are magnificently obsessed with Jesus feel a compulsion to share Him with others. Have you ever noticed that when we get a good deal on buying something, or find a bargain at the mall, or know a good place to shop or eat, we want to share it? When we have been on a trip where the scenery is breathtaking, the climate soothing, and the atmosphere exciting, we want to tell others. The truth of the matter is that Jesus is more than a good deal. His kingdom is breathtaking. His love and His life are exciting. Yet we are often timid about sharing this good news of grace, when we eagerly share the good news about our other adventures of life.

Let me propose some reasons why I think we often are inhibited in our witness. For one thing, we have erroneously assumed we must be perfect examples of the gospel before we try to share it. Of course we must be trying. We need to understand that we are growing; we are not yet grown. We are becoming; we have not arrived. However, if only the perfect bore witness of Jesus, then we would have no one to keep the flame alive.

Another self-imposed hindrance to our witness is feeling we must know it all. But not so! We do not have to be systematic theologians in order to bear our witness. Those early Christians had no developed doctrines which skillfully defined their faith. Yet they bore witness of the "Jesus" impact in their lives. God does not want us to tell what we do not know firsthand.

Furthermore, we may hesitate to witness because we have seen others who have been obnoxious and pushy in their efforts. We fear the oversell by promising more than what God intends to deliver. Here again we can only offer that which we know He has done for us. As the songwriter said correctly, "What He's done for others He'll do for you." With confidence we can expect God to treat others as He has treated us.

It is a non-threatening story we have to share. Paul perhaps said it best when he wrote, "While we were yet sinners Christ died for us." Look at what this means to us as well as what it means to those to whom we witness. It means that even while we are sinners now, He loves us. While we are doing devious things now to interrupt the progress of His church, He loves us. While we may be sinning against His will, He still loves us.

People who are beautifully obsessed with Jesus want to share graciously this love story with all who will listen. The bottom line of it all is the extravagant love of God, which brings us under the compelling influence of Jesus.

Look at what God has to offer every one of us. He offers more beauty than we can observe, more truth than we can grasp, more love than we can accept, more power than we can use, more gospel than we can preach, and more goodness than we can live.

What, then, will we do with this Jesus who is called the Christ? He belongs to us and we belong to Him. He is obsessed with us. Ought we not to be obsessed with Him?

REFLECTION

Several thoughts came to my mind while watching The Sound of Music *the other night for the umpteenth time. For one thing, good movies can be made that are wholesome, with plots that do not depend on sex or violence to keep them moving. Movies can be made that accent a person's convictions and commitment to what he or she believes is a higher good.*

The movie itself shows how good, decent folk can fall under the spell of a dictator. Survival for some people is their highest good and will cause them to turn on their friends when it is threatened. The Hitler movement of that era is a strong reminder of how easily we can follow a lie if it is clothed in convincing argument. How vulnerable we are to having someone tell us what to think!

The concept of a super-race at that time had almost everyone clamoring to be included. A majority of the masses bought the rhetoric with little thought as to its ethical and moral implications. To them, some folk could be eliminated for the greater good. Those who tried to take a stand for right were discredited, imprisoned, or eliminated.

The problem with trying to build a super-race or super-Christians is that some folk have to be excluded, and that is contrary to our Lord's teaching. The scripture makes a good case for "whosoever will." Perhaps one of the reasons we admire Captain Von

Trapp is because he refused to serve a system that was exclusive, ruthless, and totalitarian. He would not allow someone else to do his thinking for him.

The Lord Jesus calls us into a life of openness and love. The Holy Spirit equips us to be inclusive rather than exclusive. The kingdom of God is open to all who freely seek the Lord with all their hearts. The most pathetic people are those who depend on either a religious or a political dictator.

PRAYER

Dear Jesus,
we recognize the beauty of Your name.
We know it describes Your saving purpose.
We know there is no other name
whereby we can be saved.
For this reason
we celebrate Who You are.
We sing the name of Jesus.
We preach the name of Jesus.
We pray in the name of Jesus.

We confess that You are Lord.
Hear us as we pray our many prayers.
Forgive our sins of indifference.
Help us to be enamored
by that which is important to You.
We want to love You
with all of our hearts, minds, and souls.
Forgive us when we lose sight of others
because of our selfish preoccupation with You.
Deep down we know we cannot care for You
without caring for them.
Thank You, Jesus, for being Jesus
and for all Your name means
in terms of
joy,
peace,
and commitment.
In Your strong name we pray.
Amen.

Chapter 4

A SERVANT CHURCH

John 13:14-17; Acts 6:1-7; Philippians 2:5-8

One of the favorite characters of fantasyland is Cinderella. The story of Cinderella appeals to most people because we like for virtue to be rewarded. We like for good things to happen to good people and bad things to happen to bad people. We love the story of Cinderella because the prince loved her and carried her off to a beautiful castle.

I wonder, however, how a different scenario would have affected the popularity of the story. What if the loving prince, instead of taking Cinderella to a castle to live in luxury, had chosen rather to join her in the kitchen to scour and scrub? I am afraid that kind of ending would not have had great appeal.

Sometimes I think we have a Cinderella concept of the church. We want a castle, when in reality we are called to scour and scrub. The church as the bride of Christ is not called to a fantasyland of unreality, but the Christ of God wishes to join us in the kitchen.

The New Testament is full of words which teach us that the role of servanthood is God's design for every Christian. The New Testament writers use such terms as *commitment, sacrifice, surrender, martyrdom, self-giving,* and other similar words which define the

49

kind of life into which Christ has called us.

It's not an easy matter to be humble servants, because servanthood cuts across the grain of our human ego. Our selfish tendency is to share life's spotlight with no one. Our restless conceit keeps us competing with anyone who threatens our personal domain.

In Christ, however, we grow toward servanthood. We crucify our pride; we slay our competitive spirit. We die to self so that our newness in Christ can be obvious. Servanthood is very demanding, but from it we sing of a "sweet, sweet spirit in this place," and we know it comes from Christ Himself.

In the cartoon strip "Peanuts," Lucy has just set up her free counseling service for the frustrated and problem-beset folk. Charlie Brown comes to her for advice. Somehow life for him is not as meaningful as it should be. Lucy responds, "Charlie Brown, life is like a great ship on a voyage. Many kinds of people are on this ship together. Some put their deck chairs on the front of the ship to see where they are going. Others sit in their deck chairs on the back of the ship to see where they've been. Now, Charlie Brown, you need to decide in which group you belong." Charlie Brown replies, "My problem is that I have never been able to get my deck chair unfolded."

Perhaps this is a picture of the church today. Too many of us are still fumbling with our spiritual deck chairs. We are not really sure of the meaning of discipleship. We are not clear on our definition of church. We fumble with Bible study, prayer, worship, and ministry which never really open up into the fullness we long for in Christ Jesus. Perhaps we have misunderstood the call of Christian servanthood and we have basically rejected the role of servant.

Our pride and self-centered egos make it impossible for us to wash anyone's feet. Our deep-seated insecurities will not let us take anything off anybody. Nobody is going to tell us anything. "Who does the preacher think he is, trying to talk us deacons into family ministry? Doesn't he know we're supposed to sit back and make important decisions?" "Nobody's going to tell us church members we ought to visit, or tithe, or witness, or get all dirty down at that rescue mission. Let those mission enthusiasts do that dirty work." "They said they wanted us to go on youth retreat. I told them we had raised our children. Let everyone else get their own 'young-uns' grown."

Our problem is we are denying our servanthood. We want God, but we want Him on our own terms. Wilbur Rees expressed it well when he wrote, "I would like to buy three dollars' worth of God, please. Not enough to explode my soul or to disturb my sleep, but just enough to equal a cup of warm milk or a snooze in the sunshine. I don't want enough of Him to make me love a person of another race or pick beets with a migrant worker. I want ecstasy, not transformation. I want the warmth of the womb, not a new birth. I want a pound of the eternal in a paper sack. I'd like to buy three dollars' worth of God, please."

One of the things that impresses us about the post-Pentecost church was its sense of servanthood. Its members lived in close proximity to the death and resurrection of Jesus. They had a wonderful inspiration toward humble submission. With Calvary in the back of their minds, they had all the example they needed of self-giving love. Therefore, they marched across their pagan world, not so much as conquerors but as the conquered. They were not know-it-alls. They were learners, or disciples. They were not spiritually superior; they were sinners saved by grace. Their attitude and lifestyle were those of beggars trying to tell a hungry humanity where they could all find some bread.

There are several dispositions that leap out at us as we try to understand the meaning of our own servanthood in the context of a servant church. One of the first dispositions is that of *humility*. The dictionary defines *humility* as "a modest sense of one's own significance," and that is good as far as it goes.

Christian humility, however, is related to who we are in Christ. It is a gift of the Holy Spirit. It is a part of our preparation and involvement in service. Cheap, manufactured humility is more repulsive than honest arrogance. Genuine humility is never something we seek to advertise, and yet it is part of that light which must not be hidden under a bushel.

Jesus was never impressed with those who wanted to be a part of the religious parade. Yet He rebuked those pitiful souls who refused to become involved. While Christian humility ignores those who are spiritually proud, it is embarrassed by those who feel too "humble" to do anything. Humility is related to serving. If we have humility just for humility's sake, we are nothing but spiritual prudes. Godly humility conditions us to be a servant people. There is no way you and I can be humble and not be involved in some measure in serving humanity.

John Claypool gives us a good example of humility. He invites our attention to the Upper Room during the Last Supper. At one point in the happenings of that night, Jesus took a towel and a basin and washed the disciples' feet. This was a menial chore usually done at the door by a servant as guests entered. They apparently had no such servant at this gathering. It was up to someone else to do it if indeed it were to be done.

But why Jesus? He was the only one emotionally and spiritually equipped to do it. The disciples were busy fussing about who would be the greatest, or who would sit on the right hand or the left hand of our Lord. When your goal is to rise above your peers, you are not about to lower yourself in their eyes. Jesus was the only one in that room not caught up in the game of "who's going to be 'king of the mountain'?" He was the only one whose humility allowed him to serve.

Christian humility comes when we adequately deal with who we are and Whose we are. John said in his gospel, "Jesus, knowing that He came from the

Father and that He was going to the Father, began to wash their feet." In other words, Jesus knew who He was. True humility comes from understanding the eternal dimensions of our being. When God becomes a dominant factor in our self-understanding, humility emerges.

Therefore, we go forth to serve not where there is the most glory, but where there is the greatest need. When we are free from the anxiety of having to *be* something, then we can truly *do* something. Humility allows us to be servants.

Another disposition involved in defining servanthood is *brokenness*. In many ways, brokenness is closely related to humility. However, brokenness goes a step further in helping us to express and understand our servant role. Hopefully many of us are humble, at least to some degree, but few of us know much about brokenness. Humility may give us a proper opinion of ourselves, but brokenness helps us to demonstrate a humble spirit at the deepest level of our beings.

How do we understand brokenness? Our best explanation comes from the Bible. In the Bible there are two kinds of servants mentioned. First, there were the *hired* servants, who received wages and had certain rights. Then there were *bond* servants, who received no wages and had no rights. In the New Testament, the word for *servant* is almost always *bond* servant. That is, he or she had no rights, for the servant was the absolute property of the master.

Here, then, is the essence of brokenness for us. We have no rights. We belong to Him. When we are misunderstood, misrepresented, mistreated, unforgiven, left out, and hurt, we remember that Jesus "made Himself of no reputation and became obedient unto death, even the death of the cross." Brokenness is a prerequisite to servanthood. People who are always demanding their rights will never become servants. Life will not always deal with us kindly. Our service for Christ will not always produce rewards. Sometimes there will be penalties. If we become bitter and resentful and want to fight back, we lose our servanthood. It is a broken and contrite heart that God will always use. Brokenness conditions us to be bond servants. When we blend our servanthoods together, we become a servant church.

A third disposition expressed in being a servant church is *kindness*. Kindness has to do with attitude. Kindness is the spirit with which we approach our servanthood. Our most generous efforts are to no avail if they are not in keeping with the kindly character of Christ.

There is a time when right is wrong, and that is when kindness is absent. When love and compassion are not evident in our ministry, we have no ministry.

One of my seminary professors tells the story that, as a young pastor, he felt his church was not responding very well. He decided to prepare and preach a stem-winding sermon that would set everybody straight. He worked long and hard on it.

55

He felt it was just right.

Sunday morning came, and he preached with great fervor. He roared with firmness. The people listened with fear and trembling. A strange silence fell over the congregation, and the people left a bit stunned by his thunderous exhortation.

Going home that day, he could hardly wait to get his wife's response to his well-prepared, well-delivered, and attentively received sermon. When asked what she thought, his wife responded, "If there was anything Christian about that sermon, I didn't recognize it." Ouch! There is a time when right is wrong.

In Mark's gospel a certain scribe confessed to Jesus that the greatest commandment is to love God with all our understanding, soul, and strength, and our neighbor as ourselves. Jesus responded by saying, "You are not far from the kingdom." The man was not in it, but he was very close. There are times when we may know the right answers, but we must likewise have the right spirit.

There is a time, however, when right is right. It is when it takes the form of a servant. It is when rightness and kindness come together. It is one thing to be right *technically*. It is a blessed thing to be right *spiritually*. Only in our kindness can we be true servants of our living Lord.

Perhaps our question is a personal one. How is it with our lives? One day we shall all stand before our Maker, and we shall wish to hear His most desirable words. They will not be "Well done, thou great financier." He will not commend us for being great educators and preachers. He will not say, "Well done, thou great athlete, thou great church administrator, thou great salesman, thou great church worker." His most desirable words will be "Well done, thou good and faithful servant."

So, then, how well do we serve? Is our goal to be a servant church?

REFLECTION

The church of our Lord Christ was never intended to be a "bless me" club or a refrigerator to keep saints from spoiling. It was not God's major concern that church should be only an ambulance coming along behind, picking up the wounded, applying spiritual bandages, and soothing hurt feelings. The sacrificial implications of being church are well-documented in the scriptures. For this reason the church is not a gathering of spiritual prima donnas who must have their way on every issue and who think their thoughts are the only correct ones.

The church is not an art gallery where Christians, like finished statues, are set up for display. It certainly is not a convention to which each family sends a delegate. Church is a fellowship of faithful followers of Jesus who claim no spiritual superiority. It is a school for the unlearned and the imperfect. There is so much to know and so far to grow that no one who is truly spiritual will dare look down on the spirituality of others. Everyone's motives are so fickle and faulty at times it ill behooves anyone to assume his or her intentions are always pure.

Church is a training camp to mold people into the pattern of our Lord's perfect character. His gentle nature toward hurting humanity and His stern disposition toward a false religiosity are a balance church folk seek to achieve. Nowhere is the spirit of Jesus less obvious than among church people who become nervous and critical about peripheral matters.

Church is a kind of spiritual laboratory where committed Christians experiment with such things as love, grace, repentance, forgiveness, and the total art of living under the Lordship of Jesus. No one has all the answers and no one does it best all the time. There is a bit of trial and error in the way church functions. Some things are launched in faith, trusting God for accuracy and accomplishment. When things go well we give God the glory. When they do not go well we go back to the "laboratory" and find the ingredients for a more godly approach. The exciting thing about church is that we have a fellowship in which we can "fail" forward.

Whatever else church is, it is not a hammock for the lazy. It is a well-fitted yoke which enables us to pull together for Jesus Christ. "Blest be the tie that binds our hearts in Christian love."

PRAYER

Lord, You have served us well as
Creator,
Provider,
and Savior.
You have invested much in our lives,
for which we are grateful.
You have loved us
before we were capable of loving You.
You had a plan for us
even before we were ever planned.
You called us
long before we were ever listening.

Now, O Lord, we wish to return to You
something of that which You have inspired within us.
We want to be a servant people
even as You have been a servant God.
Teach us, Lord, how to imitate Jesus
in the doing of Your will.
May our pride
be lost in His humility.
May our hearty, aggressive natures
give way to His brokenness.
May our hostilities
be dissolved in His kindness.
Bless us, O Lord, in such a way
that we in turn
may be a blessing to others.
Thank You for giving us church
as a vehicle for serving You
by serving others.
Amen.

Chapter 5

LIFE IS A MINISTRY

Genesis 12:1-3; Matthew 25:34-40

The meaning of ministry begins with an understanding of God and what He is doing in His world. Early in the Old Testament we get the idea that God was vitally interested in the affairs of humankind. God created man and woman with the awesome capacity to be free. In their freedom they chose to rebel, and the rebellion separated them from God. Therefore, God began a process of reconciling humankind unto Himself. He took the initiative in trying to lift us from our fallen state of existence.

The genesis, or the beginning, of ministry centers in God's redemptivity. In the call of Abraham and the establishing of a chosen nation, it is evident that God wanted to use people to perform His purpose. God wanted Israel to become a nation of ministers to the entire world. For the most part, they did not fulfill their mission and became a disappointment to God.

In the New Testament we find that God was in Christ reconciling the world unto Himself. Jesus saw this task of reconciliation as closely related to healing the sick, comforting the poor and bereaved, loving the sinful and outcast, and teaching the learners. In Jesus Christ we understand best what God is doing in His world.

The New Testament not only tells us what Jesus was doing, but also what He wants us to do. We call this "ministry." In the New Testament, Christians are called "a royal priesthood." In calling us priests, the New Testament implies that we have a ministry. In fact, the Christian life is a ministry. Unless you and I are willing to accept a ministry, we are not ready to accept Christ in the fullest sense. Unless we are willing to become involved with people and life, we have no ministry.

The question arises, however, What does ministry look like? What does it sound like? What does it feel like? It is one thing to call ourselves ministers; it is something else for each of us to act like we have a ministry.

Christian ministry means that in all of life's situations we respond like Jesus. Let us focus on four words which we shall call "the vocabulary of ministry" because they are vital to our participation in it.

The first word is *care*. Other words could have been used, such as *love, compassion, concern*, the Greek word *agape*, or some similar term. The word *care* is a good word because it speaks to our times. We are a people on the verge of losing our capacity to care.

Near the end of His ministry Jesus was in the temple lamenting the religious conditions of His people. His remarks were mostly centered at scribes and Pharisees, as indicated in Matthew 23. He left the temple in a mood of concern and predicted its destruction.

Later the disciples wanted further explanation of His strange words. Matthew recorded His explanation in chapter 24. Jesus said there would be the appearance of men claiming to be the Christ. There would be wars and rumors of wars, famines, earthquakes, persecution, hatred, and false prophets. But in verse 12 He said, "Because of the spread of wickedness, the love of many will grow cold."

One of the terrible things which characterizes our world today is a lack of genuine concern. With pockets of poverty in our affluent cities, crimes of every description spiraling across our land, and spiritual needs all around us, most of us sit back waiting for some government agency to come to the rescue. All the while we are losing our capacity for personal compassion.

Some of us contribute generously to benevolent institutions and United Fund-like causes. This is good, but it can keep us an arm's length from real ministry. Our giving is indispensable, yet we must not use it to avoid our own personal crosses. It is possible to develop a kind of polite indifference which tends to smother our sympathy and paralyze our capacity to care.

The essential ingredient, and perhaps a weakening ingredient, in ministry today is caring. Caring is the essence of Christianity. Paul reminded us of this in I Corinthians 13 when he emphasized that if we do not care, we are nothing.

Caring and loving are the greatest things in the world, but it is awful when they grow cold. This is why we need church, with its weekly worship and Christian fellowship. It helps keep our love warm. It keeps the fires of our compassion burning. It keeps our care kindled. *Care* is indeed a strong word in the definition of ministry.

A second word vitally related to ministry is not a familiar word, but a good one. It is *empathy*. To empathize means to enter into the feeling or the spirit of another person. It means to fully identify with someone else.

A beautiful expression of empathy is found in the Old Testament. The nation of Judah was in Babylonian captivity. They were a sad and lonely people. Ezekiel was called of God to be the pastor/prophet among those lifeless exiles. In the third chapter of the book which bears his name, he gave a hint as to his personal preparation for the assignment. He said, "I sat where they sat."

When seen against the background of Israel's historical predicament, this is a profound statement. What he is saying is that he identified with his people. He sat where they sat. He bled through their veins. He hurt their kind of hurt. He shared their kind of homesickness. He wept their kind of tears. This is empathy at its best.

It may be possible that in our kind of world we are losing our ability to be empathetic. Because the mass media has given us a front-row seat to all the

64

horrors and atrocities in the world, nothing shocks us anymore. It's possible that our hyper-exposure to tragedy has made us insensitive to the hurting edge of life. We tend to forget those people whose misfortunes make the headlines today. Yet many of those same folk live out the remainder of their lives in quiet desperation.

Our world is full of people who need us to cry with them, laugh with them, hurt with them, and feel with them. If we learn to build defenses against our feelings, we can empathize with no one. As a result, we will have no real ministry with anyone. *Empathy* is indeed a big word in defining ministry.

The third word in our interpretation of ministry is *involvement*. To be involved in ministry is to be able to use our creative ingenuities, the power of our personalities, and the energy of our lives in helping God do His thing in His world. To be involved means to be conscious of people and their needs. It means to live in the "now"--not in the past or in the future, but in the "right now."

To be involved in ministry is to give ourselves to the present moment and to the people with whom we share this moment. Have you ever been talking to someone who kept looking at his or her watch, fretting about the next hour or a later appointment? You never had this person's attention because he or she was living in the future. Most of us live that way. We never give enough of ourselves to the present moment so that we can exert a healing influence on others.

To live in the "now" is to be able to love and care for every person who crosses our paths. One reason Jesus was so effective was that He lived in the "now." There were no big days or little days in His life. Every day was a big event. Whether He was casting evil spirits from a Gadarene demoniac or talking to a rich young ruler about eternal life, He gave the best of Himself to every moment and to every person He encountered. Thus came the children and the centurions, the publicans and the rulers of the Jews. The fishermen and the farmers came, as well as the harlots and the sinners. They all came and were treated as sons and daughters of God.

The story is told of a busy executive who was rushing to catch a train in New York City. He had decided that very morning that he would really try to *be* a Christian instead of just talking about being one. By the time he had picked up his ticket, he was late. He went charging across the lobby with his bags as he heard the last call, "All aboard." He was on the ramp, about to get on the train, when he bumped into a small child with his suitcase. The little boy had been carrying a jigsaw puzzle. The pieces were now scattered all over the platform.

The busy executive paused, saw the child in tears, and, with an inward sigh, stopped, smiled, and helped the boy pick up his puzzle as the train pulled out of the station. The child watched him intently. When they had finished picking up the pieces, the little boy looked at the man with a kind of awe and said,

"Mister, are you Jesus?" For that moment the man realized that on that platform to that little boy on that day, he was.

It happens that way when we live in the "now" and when we give ourselves to every moment. When seen in the light of our dealings with other people, *involvement* is a strong part of the vocabulary of ministry.

The fourth word in our vocabulary of ministry is *vulnerability*. This word describes our willingness to take the risks involved in ministry. One of the consequences of genuine Christian ministry is that we can be hurt. If we allow ourselves to care and feel deeply about others and if we get involved in their lives, we run the risk of being misunderstood and rejected. People to whom we give ourselves can betray us and become a disappointment. Ministry at its best is allowing ourselves to be used and, at times, redemptively abused for the sake of others.

This does not mean, however, that as Christians we become a kind of passive doormat on which the world wipes its feet. It does mean that we turn the other cheek, walk the second mile, and forgive "seventy times seven" on behalf of others.

When we take our ministry seriously and begin to love the unlovely, witness to the outcast, and refuse to reflect the popular hostilities and prejudices of our community, we will be hated. It takes courage to care enough to become vulnerable.

For example, we become vulnerable when we

love someone enough to marry them and when we bring children into the world. These people whom we love more than our own lives can disappoint and hurt us at times. We become vulnerable when we take Jesus seriously because He calls us into the kind of life in which we can be wounded.

The alternative is not to get involved. Do not rock the boat. Do not have any convictions that go against the grain of the status quo. Play it cool. Do your own thing. Don't love. Don't care. Don't let your sympathy go wild, and you will avoid a lot of pain.

A few years ago Paul Simon expressed this approach to life in a song entitled "I Am a Rock." Some of the lines went like this: "I am a rock, I am an island. . . . I have no need of friendship; friendship causes pain. It's laughter and it's loving I disdain. . . . If I never loved, I never would have cried. . . . I am shielded in my armor, hiding in my room, and safe within my womb. I touch no one and no one touches me. I am a rock; I am an island. And a rock feels no pain, and an island never cries."

This song is not true. This is not the way to live. It's true we cannot die if we are not alive, but who wants to be a rock? Only as we become vulnerable and willing to expose ourselves to all the hurt and risks of caring can we truly find life. Whatever else hell may be, it must be isolation and loneliness. It must be "cut-offness," where God is not received and everyone cries in agony, "I am a rock; I am an island."

Albert Camus, in his novel entitled *The Fall*, tells of a prominent French lawyer. As a young man he had refused to risk his life to save a drowning woman one night. Years later he was drinking heavily in a barroom. He was overheard talking to himself and saying, "Oh, young woman, young woman, please throw yourself into the water again so that I might have a second chance to save both of us."

Yes, it hurts to care. It hurts to take risks. But here is where we find the meaning of our personhood. Here is where God is. In ministry we may hurt, but not as those who have no hope. *Vulnerability* must be included in our understanding of authentic ministry.

In no way have we completely defined the awesome meaning of ministry. If we learn anything from the Bible, we learn that life is a ministry. This means that in giving us life, God has given us a task. We are not spectators on this planet Earth. We are not immune to difficulties and sorrows. We cannot escape the fact that we are brothers and sisters, and that we are one another's keepers. You and I are responsible *to* each other and *for* each other and for others, and this is our ministry.

REFLECTION

In the heart of God there is a special love for all humankind. It is a love which seeks only that which is best for those created in His image. This love never falters in its appeal for truth, beauty, and goodness. It is more than a synthetic emotion. It is greater than amorous words. It is deeper than theological debate. This love has a capacity to die for those He loves; yet, it inspires life at its best.

This love is beyond human definition. It required an act of grace, which was a visit from God Himself, to translate this love into life. Our best word for God's amazing grace is Jesus. Our most important response to its appeal is commitment. Such love has the power to energize us for godly assignments.

In the mind of God there is a special plan for this love to be made known to all the world. It is a plan which requires the efforts of everyone who believes Jesus is the Son of God. We call it "missions." God does not zap the world into submission by His mighty power, but rather He has chosen to love the world through everyone who has grasped the light of His love. It is a "people" plan where God trusts human ingenuity and commitment to get the Word into the hearts of needy folk. The extent to which we neglect our assignment is the extent to which God's plan is weakened. We have an awesome responsibility to share God's love with a pagan world. We must make Christ known with as much ability as we have to do so.

We are not left alone, however, for this gigantic task because in the hands of God are the divine resources for reaching our world. We have the power of His purpose, the push of His presence, and the promise that all things will work for good to those who love God and are called according to His purpose. Thus we are without excuse if we allow our missionary zeal to waver.

God has equipped us to be His people and to share His love from here to the ends of the earth. Let us celebrate all the ways God has reached out in love to us and the ways we, can reach out to others.

PRAYER

Our prayer to You today, O Lord,
is about ministry.
Thank You for calling us
to be a kingdom of priests.
Thank You for trusting us
to care for one another.

Give us, O Lord,
the skills for ministry
as well as the desire for it.
We want to feel what others feel.
We want to identify
with their sorrows and successes.
Give us the courage to get involved
even though it makes us vulnerable.
Thank You, Lord,
for people who have ministered to us.
We know You have loved us
through the efforts of others.
Help us to pass this grace along
to those with whom we share life.
Even now, we pray, O Lord,
for those who will cross our paths today.
Help us to be alert
to whatever opportunities we have for ministry.
May those who are sick
find healing
and those who are dying
find comfort.
May the lonely find friendship
and the lost find the Lord.
May love find us all
as ministers to one another.
Amen.

Chapter 6

EVERY BELIEVER A PRIEST

Exodus 19:3-8; I Peter 2:1-9

For years, preaching professor Fred Craddock went back to his hometown in West Tennessee for Christmas. Every year he visited his old friend Buck, who owned the cafe on Main Street. Each year Buck would give Dr. Craddock a cup of coffee and a piece of chess pie.

One year when Craddock went for his coffee and pie, Buck said, "Let's go out and get your coffee across the street."

"What's wrong with here?" Craddock replied. "Is this not a restaurant anymore?"

"Sometimes I wonder," Buck responded.

Later, as they sat sipping coffee, Buck began to talk. "Did you see the curtain?" he asked Craddock.

"Oh, yes, I saw the curtain. I always see the curtain," was Craddock's comment.

The curtain separated the front half of the restaurant from the back. White folk came in the front and black folk came in the back.

"The curtain has to go," said Buck.

"That is good," said Craddock.

"Oh, that's easy for you to say," said Buck. "If I take the curtain down and treat black folk like white folk, I lose my business. But if I leave it up, I lose my soul."

The doctrine of the priesthood of believers is about curtains coming down. Matthew tells us that on the cross, Jesus cried with a loud voice and yielded up His spirit, and the veil, or the curtain, of the temple was torn in two from top to bottom.

The temple curtain symbolized many separations. It symbolized the separation of people from God. It symbolized the separation of religious leaders from the worshipers. It symbolized the separation of females from males. It symbolized the separation of Gentiles from Jews. It symbolized the separation of the secular from the sacred. It symbolized the separation of the priests from the people.

The torn temple curtain means that now every believer is a priest. We do not have to go through someone else to get to God. We do not have to let someone else do church for us. As believers, we are all called to be ministers. The responsibility for the lost world is on all our shoulders. The curtain is torn; therefore, God deals with each of us as individuals.

True authority belongs to God. Therefore, no pope, no dictator preacher, and no church power-clique has the right to dominate our spiritual thoughts. The temple curtain is torn, and that means we do not have to put up with bad religion. We do not have to put up with bad preaching and church people who clear off a spot and pitch a fit if they don't get their way. The temple curtain is torn, and now we have a priesthood of all believers.

One of the vitally important ideas and distinctive doctrines accented by the Reformation was the fact that every believer is a priest. The entire spirit of the Reformation was an attempt to recapture the New Testament emphasis on a personal encounter with God through faith in Jesus Christ.

The problem the Reformation leaders had with the Catholic church was that it had placed itself between man and God. The church had erected another temple curtain. It had taken away the individual's access to God. The church was ignoring the people of God by placing religious authority in church officers rather than the leadership of the Holy Spirit. Church members had become religious puppets manipulated by the strings of a dictatorial church.

Could it be that today we need to recapture the spirit of the Reformation in this vital teaching of the New Testament? It might just be that we have neglected this precious concept of individual priesthood until we have found ourselves drifting toward the same pattern of sixteenth-century Catholicism. Like they, we have over-institutionalized the church.

Nowadays, church is more of a place to go rather than a people on the go. Church members are more like spectators than the participants which our Lord expects. The word *layperson* is almost synonymous with *amateur*. Perhaps we need another reformation, or at least we definitely need to understand, accept, and appreciate our priesthood in Christ Jesus.

As we consider this topic, let us review its biblical origin. The idea of priesthood goes back into the Old Testament, where we see it as a vital part of Hebrew religion. The priesthood was expected to protect the purity and the integrity of Israel. The priests were ministers of the Lord, and they were mediators between man and God. The Hebrew word for *priest* projected this person as one who related to and acted for God.

Although the Old Testament pictures the priesthood as an organized group of worship leaders, it also presents the idea that all of Israel were to be priests. Look at Exodus 19:3-8. It says:

> Then Moses went up unto God, and the Lord called to him from the mountain and said, "This is what you are to say to the house of Jacob and what you are to tell the people of Israel: 'You yourselves have seen what I did to Egypt, and how I carried you on eagles' wings and brought you to myself. Now if you obey me fully and keep my covenant, then out of all nations you will be my treasured possession. Although the whole earth is mine, you will be for me a kingdom of priests and a holy nation.' These are the words which you are to

speak to the Israelites." So Moses went back and summoned the elders of the people and set before them all the words the Lord had commanded him to speak. The people all responded together, "We will do everything the Lord has said." So Moses brought their answer back to the Lord.

This was God's invitation to His people to be priests. Notice their response was "We will do it." Apparently, in God's mind from the beginning, there was the idea of every believer being a priest.

Peter picked up on this idea as he described the Christian community in I Peter 2:9, which says, "But you are a chosen people, a royal priesthood, a holy nation, a people belonging to God, that you may declare the praises of Him who called you out of darkness into His marvelous light." First-century Christians applied Exodus 19:6 to themselves. Thus, the priesthood of Israel became the priesthood of believers.

Another significant feature of biblical priesthood was the place of the high priest. He was the chief religious person. On the day of atonement, he entered the holy of holies. This was a place inside the temple, separated and hidden from the people by the veil, or the curtain. Only this person was allowed to enter the holy of holies to make atonement for the sins of the people.

When Jesus died on the cross, He became the sacrifice of all sacrifices. He became the High Priest of all high priests for our sins. We need no other high priest anymore, nor any other sacrifice, for that matter. When the veil of the temple tore, there was no longer a holy of holies where we cannot go. Through Jesus as our high priest, we all have the right to plead our cases to God.

It is significant to understand that in the New Testament, the term *priest* was never used to refer to the clergy or ordained leaders. The priesthood belonged to all believers.

This biblical origin and understanding of the priesthood give us a background for Christian priesthood today. Let us focus on two major meanings.

First of all, its most obvious meaning is, as believers, we all have direct access to God. No human mediator is necessary. Salvation is not a matter between you and your friends, between you and your pastor, or between you and your church. It is between you and your Lord. This puts religion on a personal basis. Our contact with God becomes a matter of personal friendship.

Because we have access to God, we can seek His forgiveness every day. We can claim His promises every hour. We can have the calm assurance of His presence in all of life's circumstances. God is available. What a discovery!

Because we have direct access to God, we have the right to read and interpret the scriptures for ourselves as the Spirit leads. The responsibility to learn and to grow is part of our Christian priesthood. We have a capacity to understand and to have an opinion. When one person or group of persons tries to coerce others to interpret the Bible exactly as they do, then the priesthood of believers is seriously violated.

A second major meaning of the priesthood of believers is, as a priest, every Christian has a ministry to perform. From the New Testament perspective, this concept is not seen as a lighthearted idea to tickle the ears of inquisitive saints. It is a serious doctrine that has its roots in the eternal purpose of God.

The Christian life is a ministry with a calling from God and is under the judgment of God. Too long we have equated the ministry of the church with what the pastor or the staff is doing. If you are a child of God and if you are a sincere believer, then you are a priest, regardless of how insignificant you may feel. You are a priest, regardless of how spiritually illiterate you may be or how busy you may seem.

If a church is to ever realize its dream, then its ministry must extend far beyond that of staff and a handful of committed leaders. It must be extended through every personality within its membership. This is the heart of the doctrine of the priesthood of believers.

What, then, is this ministry? I Peter 2:5 says, "You are a holy priesthood, offering spiritual sacrifices." *Holy* here does not imply a self-righteous preoccupation with one's personal goodness. It describes Christian maturity expressed in a sincere love for people. *Offering spiritual sacrifices* means putting away all malice, insincerity, evil, and slander. We sacrifice our pride because holiness is not haughtiness. It is a love for people. Our spiritual sacrifices enable us to love others.

In I Peter 2:9, it says we are a royal priesthood, where the emphasis is on *praise*. We praise our Lord by the way we worship and by the way we witness. Paul says it another way in II Corinthians 5:18: "All this is of God, who reconciled us to Himself through Christ and gave us the ministry of reconciliation."

This means that as Christian priests, we are called to reconcile, not divide. We are called to heal, and not to hurt. We are called to forgive, and not antagonize. We are called to love, and not hate. To save, and not destroy.

The Latin word for *priest* is *pontifex*. It means "bridge-builder." Our Christian priesthood calls us to build some bridges and help people to God and to one another. We are to make intercession, not only in prayer, but by the way we act. We help create a climate of reconciliation when we exercise our proper priesthood.

Dr. Bruce Larson tell about riding home on a bus one day which was so crowded many were standing, as he was. The bus made a sudden turn and threw him into a man seated. It was a hard blow, and Bruce apologized. The man, however, became irate and created a scene on the bus. His anger would not let him hear Bruce's continued apologies.

A young man seated next to the angry rider tried to calm him, but to no avail. A lady tried to defend Bruce by telling the man the whole thing was unavoidable. Several people got involved. Some took sides with the man; others took sides with Bruce. Two nuns sat quietly in front, reading their books.

At the next stop, the angry man got off, and even he jostled someone on the way out. Bruce then took his seat beside the young man. Bruce asked the young man if the angry man was his friend. He replied, "No, I never saw him before, but he did tell me he had lost his job today. That is why he was so rude to you. I hope you will forgive him."

Dr. Larson said it occurred to him that in every such episode of misunderstanding, there is a similar cast of characters. There is the offender, who was Bruce himself; there is the offended, which was the angry man; there are the side-takers, represented by the woman and the others who made comments; there are the uninvolved, represented by the nuns sitting quietly in the front of the bus. But hopefully, there is a priest. He or she is a mediator--a bridge-builder--and that was the young man who tried to bring about reconciliation. This young man tried to remove the barriers of misunderstanding.

The profound question we need to ask ourselves is, What do we do in a similar circumstance? Are we peacemakers, or are we troublemakers? If we are troublemakers, we will never fulfill our priesthood.

As believers, you and I are called to be priests. We have direct access to God for ourselves, and we have a terrific responsibility for others. Our Lord invites us into a ministry of love and reconciliation.

I once read about a seven-year-old boy who had only one arm. He had lost his left arm in an accident. He came to Sunday School one Sunday as a visitor. The teacher often ended the class by having the pupils make a "hand" church. They would put their hands together and say, "Here's the church, and here's the steeple; open the door and there are the people." Realizing that the amputee visitor had only one hand, a seven-year-old girl moved across the aisle and stood beside him. She put her left hand to his only hand, saying, "We'll make the church by putting our hands together."

In reality, that's how we do church, and that's how we do our priesthood. We put our hands together and reach out to a needy world.

REFLECTION

Through the centuries, Christianity has tended to place varying degrees of emphasis upon the laity. The extent to which laypeople have been involved in the leadership and direction of the church has depended upon close adherence to the New Testament pattern. The spirit of reformation and renewal has always called for broader participation. To put the control and the impact of the church only in the hands of the professional clergy is to sow the seeds of its eventual decline.

Jesus said, "If you hold to my teaching ... then you will know the truth, and the truth will set you free." Freedom-loving people will always require a place of involvement in the total process of being the people of God. It is a violation of holy scripture and human personality to inhibit the genuine thoughts and spiritual energies of the laity. There is no way to have the rule of the Holy Spirit within the church if we exclude the input of a vast segment of the body of Christ.

Of course, there can develop among the laity a religious lethargy which allows a spiritual hierarchy to emerge. When church people are unwilling to think and pray and study for themselves, there is always someone waiting to emerge as their spiritual dictator. Religion, like politics, has a terrible capacity for corruption. Perhaps its greatest guarantee for purity is that the people of God find themselves led by the

Spirit to perform the work of Christ in a world of need.

Nothing can inhibit disintegration within the church like broad participation in the tasks of witness and ministry. Nothing encourages this participation like the recognition and appreciation of each member's call to Christian priesthood. Therefore, let us rise up to be a people of faith whose authority flows from God and His Word rather than from human opinion or personal ambition. Only eternity will reveal the powerful impact of a church whose laity have truly learned and committed themselves to being church.

PRAYER

Thank You, Lord,
for empowering us to be a priestly people.
You have invited us to call upon You,
and our prayer is one of intercession.
We ask that You be as gracious to others
as You have been to us.
Reach out Your hand of healing
and touch our sin-sick world.

*Speak gently the words of truth
to each troubled mind.
Guide the lost and lonely
by the light of Your love.
Comfort the uncomfortable
with Your "Peace, be still."
Teach us, Lord,
the lessons of our priestly role.
Give us listening ears
for those who cry.
Equip us to care
for those in need.
Help us to bear the burdens
of those who are weary.
May we sense Your presence
as we share our presence with others.
We believe in You
and You believe in us
and for that faith we are grateful.
Amen.*

Chapter 7

WHAT IS THAT IN YOUR HAND?

Romans 12:1-8; I Corinthians 1:26-31

A young man got up early one Sunday morning, but instead of going to church, he went fishing. As he returned home in the afternoon, he faced a dilemma. In his hands was a string of three prize bass. Down the street came the pastor. He greeted Bobby with this comment: "I did not see you in church today, did I?"

"No, sir," was his reply.

"What is that in your hand?" the pastor asked.

With a stroke of genius the young man replied, "Pastor, just look at the trouble these fish got into for biting on Sunday!"

On a more serious note, however, the question is, What is that in *your* hand? God often comes to us seeking an answer to that question. It is as though He wants us to see the value of who we are and what we have.

The question has been asked of men and women through the centuries. Moses had a rod, and God used it to demonstrate to him and to the people of Israel the power of His purpose.

As you may recall, Moses was a fugitive from Egyptian justice and had settled in the land of Midian. There God called him from a phenomenal burning bush to go back to Egypt and lead his people out. Of course, Moses objected and offered numerous excuses. He had no standing in Egypt. He had no gifts for such a task. The whole matter was too unreasonable for the people in Egypt to believe.

God's response to Moses was in the form of a question. "What is that in your hand, Moses?" "Just a rod--my shepherd's rod," came the reply. "Throw it on the ground," said God. Moses complied, and it became a serpent wiggling in the dust. God commanded Moses to pick it up. Cautiously he did, and it became a rod again.

We follow this rod as it was used to help persuade a reluctant Pharaoh to let God's people go. It was used as an instrument of God for the parting of the Red Sea. It was used in the defeat of the Amalekites and other miracles of God. Just a shepherd's rod, but, oh, so much more in the hands of a man who was submissive to the will of God!

David had a sling in his hand, and God used it. We are familiar with that story of heroism and divine intervention. It was a sad day for the army of Israel when David took his older soldier brothers some supplies. They were doing battle with the Philistines but could not conquer them. In fact, neither side could get the advantage.

The Philistines had a giant they offered to do battle one-on-one with an Israelite. The winner would determine the outcome of the battle. Of course, no one in Israel was a match for the oversized Goliath. There was fear in the camp which David, a naive young man, could not understand. If God was on their side, why fear anything, especially a Philistine?

As you know, he accepted the challenge, and with nothing but his sling and a mighty faith in God, he slew the giant in the name of Jehovah. Victory belonged to the army of Israel because David used what he had in his hand for the glory of God. We say, "It was just a sling." Yes, but it was so much more in the hands of a young man who dared to defy the enemy in the name of Jehovah!

A small boy had a lunch, but God used it. As you recall, Jesus had been teaching and healing all day. Thousands had congregated on the hillside to see and hear.

Mealtime came and passed. People were getting hungry. It was a long way into the village, and no one had brought a lunch. The disciples were worried. They must have moved through the crowd, searching for food. Suddenly, Andrew spotted the boy with his basket.

"What is that in your hand?"

"Five loaves and two fishes, sir," the lad replied. Andrew took the boy to Jesus, and Jesus blessed that small lunch into enough food to feed the five thousand.

All the people were fed because a young boy was willing to give what he had to Jesus. We say, "Just a lunch?" But, oh, it was so much more in the hands of a boy who was willing to give it all to Jesus!

Joseph of Arimathea had a tomb, but God used

it. It was just a family burial plot. Yet, when Jesus was crucified, there was no such place to bury Him. His precious body could not be thrown on the rubbish heap. Therefore, Joseph gave his tomb, and God used it as a place where His son overcame death, hell, and the grave.

God used the empty tomb as a tangible witness to the resurrection. Disciples and friends rushed to it to discover for themselves that the Lord was risen. "Just a burial plot," we might say. Yes, it was, but it was so much more in the hands of a man who allowed God to use his tomb in proving that death can be overcome in the power of resurrection glory!

One day outside the temple area, Peter and John were confronted by a crippled beggar. They had no silver or gold, but such as they had they gave in the name of the Lord. They shared the healing grace of God, and the man was able to walk again.

Paul had a thorn in the flesh which greatly disturbed him. He prayed on occasion for its removal; yet, he submitted that troublesome ailment to the Lord Jesus Christ. It allowed him to be a more usable servant of the Lord.

John, in prison on the island of Patmos, gave his solitude to God. Through it he gained a vision of eternal things so that people for centuries to come could catch a glimpse of heaven's glory. Neither John nor Paul whined away their misfortunes, but gave them to God to be used for His purposes.

Many are the stories of God's using what

someone had to offer. However, the bottom line of it all is, What is that in *your* hand? What do you and I have that God has a divine craving to use?

For one thing, we have a life, and to have life implies that we have meaning. God doesn't go around zapping life on people for no reason at all. There is a purpose and there is a meaning to the life God has given us. The reason you and I are alive today is because God still has a purpose for our being.

It is true we may not be fulfilling that purpose as He wishes; nonetheless, our lives are God's most valuable assets. He created us in His own image to be His representatives on this planet Earth.

We have this life in our hands. God has given it to us, but He wants it to be a God-centered life. He knows what is best for us. He who made us knows the inner function of our being. He is the most qualified to fix our sin-sick souls and give us a sense of fulfillment.

This life which God has given is enclosed in a body. It is a visible, functioning organism capable of fantastic feats. Paul says we are to "present our bodies as living sacrifices, holy and pleasing to God, which is our spiritual worship."

Worship here is more than sitting passively while others entertain us. It is our service rendered. In fact, the King James Version translated it "reasonable service." We turn this physical body into a spiritual machine. We present it, or rather, we *surrender* it, to God. That body which God has freely given us is of no value to us or Him unless He is the Lord of it.

This body in which we find ourselves has a mind. It must be renewed. It must think properly. Paul asks us to be transformed by the renewing of our minds.

All actions, good or bad, are the result of our thinking. Christianity is a religion of the mind. We do not assassinate our brains when we come to Jesus. Wisdom has always been a product of faith. Crazy stuff in the name of religion comes from minds that have not been disciplined in the things of God.

The body in which we find ourselves also has a personality. Personality is a combination of body features, mental attitude, and spiritual disposition.

We hear a lot today about *charisma*. Charisma is nothing more than personality power. Your charisma and your personality are those features which describe and define only you. When God doesn't have you, He is lacking something very unique in His kingdom.

The body which houses our life, our mind, and our personality furthermore has a will. This means we are free to do our own thing. God does not violate our wishes. Of course, we suffer the consequences of our rebellious choices. We do reap what we sow.

Yet, God invites us to surrender our will to His will. Paul said, "Let this mind be in you which was also in Christ Jesus." Only in God's will are we able to manage our choices.

What is that in your hand? It is a life. A life with a body, a mind, a personality, and a will. Does

God have your life to the extent that His miracles of grace may be performed through you?

Martin Niemoeller was a German Christian pastor during World War II. He dared to defy Hitler and ended up in a concentration camp. His life and his writings have meant much to Christians around the world.

While Niemoeller was in prison, an American pastor went to console his parents. Niemoeller's father made the following statement to that pastor: "Oh, don't pity us. We'll make it. Surely it is a bad thing to have a son in a concentration camp. But there could be something more terrible, and that would be if God needed a faithful martyr and our son Martin had been unwilling."

Another thing we have in our hands, besides our life, is a calling. In writing to the Christians at Corinth, Paul reminded them of our calling in Christ Jesus.

If we have received Christ as our Savior and Lord, we have a calling to discipleship. We have a divine assignment in God's kingdom. We cannot excuse ourselves by pleading ignorance or ineffectiveness. We have all been given the spiritual tools necessary to equip us for our tasks. We are not called because we are so great, but because we can be greatly used.

We have been called of God and we have been gifted by God. It is our responsibility to remember our call, cultivate the gift God has given, and be a positive person for the Lord Christ.

It is important for us to be a "people" church because we are all in this thing together. We have no earthly leader to exalt. We are not trying to make a name for ourselves so we can impress the religious community or overwhelm people with our genius. We are a bunch of "nobodies" being called of God to be "somebodies" for Jesus. We have nothing to prove, nothing to defend, and nothing to argue about. All we have is an authentic desire to serve others. That is our calling.

What is that in your hand? You have your life, and you have your calling. They are as powerful as Moses' rod, David's sling, the boy's lunch, and the empty tomb. Will you yield them to God? Lying out before you is your destiny, your service, and your opportunity to be God's person.

REFLECTION

My porch-side tomato plant began the season blooming, growing, and forming tiny fruit. For several weeks it seemed to sit there moving ever so slowly toward some kind of yield. It was as durable as it was patient. The heavy winds and rain beat upon it. Hail even belted it with rock-like pellets. Yet, it stood tall and proud as it braved the elements.

Its early fruit began to ripen, and their redness displayed the beauty of the plant. More blooms emerged as if to say there were more to come. They offered hope even as the hot, dry wind of midsummer began to take its toll. The lack of moisture caused lower branches to turn brown and droop downward. At the top, however, it stayed green and healthy until its last fruit had ripened. A worm helped itself to the last bit of life in the remaining leaves. Now the plant is finished and seems to say with Paul, "I have fought a good fight. I have run the race. I have kept the faith." It was true to its "tomatohood."

If we permit ourselves, we can learn a lesson from this garden plant. During its brief span of life it teaches us some valuable truths. For one thing, God's hand is upon every created species. There is a time and a season for everything. The rhythm of planting, growing, and harvest is a beautiful process to observe.

Even as the tomato plant obeyed its genetic commands, we, too, are programmed to follow God's plan. The problem with us is that we are free to disobey, and our harvest is limited to that extent. If, like the tomato, we would be true to who we are through rain or shine, storm or calm, our fruit would please our Planter. At times we may appear to be unproductive, but if we are patient and persevere, the Lord of the harvest will claim our fruit. We can survive those who want a piece of us until the end.

PRAYER

Thank You, Lord,
for allowing us to live in these days.
We have so much
for which to be grateful.
There is so much
which fascinates our imaginations.
We are surrounded by fantastic technology
and marvelous scientific miracles.
Our world is forever changing
and You have given us
front-row observation
to life in the fast lane.

95

*You have equipped us
to reach out and care
at a time when caring is in short supply.
Utilize our gifts, O Lord,
for Your glory.
Burden us
with the needs which surround us.
Bless us
with the kind of blessings
we can share with others.
Love us
with the kind of love
that is contagious.
Forgive us our failures
even as we forgive those who fail us.
Lift our spirits
when we are weary.
Give us heart
when we are lonely.
May Your peace give us hope
and Your presence give us power.
Amen.*

Chapter 8

MAKING THE MOST OF OUR TIME

Ephesians 5:15-20

Time marches on with each inevitable tick of the clock and turn of the calendar. We are extremely dependent on these devices which monitor our days. Yet, were there no such things as clocks and calendars, we would still have many reminders of the passing of time. There is evidence all around us of what time is doing to us.

Time moves on, and with it are the unavoidable changes of our human existence. Nothing stays the same. Every moment of the day has its own unique ability to be different. Transition is the way of life, and at best we learn to adjust, or we spend our years in fruitless frustration.

Whether we think about it much or not, we are all running out of time. Life is passing us by far more quickly than we can absorb it. Our lives are being crammed with agendas that grow more frustrating every day. We all seem to be faced with the exhaustion of a race we are not equipped to run. Our minds and our bodies are tired, and from the youngest of us to the oldest of us, we seem to be living on nervous energy.

No wonder we are in the midst of a drug culture. No wonder alcoholism continues to be such a national problem. These are the only ways some people feel they can escape the competitive, exhausting world in which they live. Most of us have been hitting the aspirin bottle and taking the headache remedies with far greater frequency than should be necessary. The reason is because our bodies are not equipped for the rapid pace we feel we must maintain.

We are in the process of losing ourselves in the intensity of our accelerated culture. *Tense, anxious, frustrated,* and *exhausted* are fast becoming the words which best describe us. Virginia Brasier has adequately described our modern-day dilemma with the following poem:

This is the age
Of the half-read page.
And the quick hash
And the mad dash.
The bright night
With the nerves tight.
The plane hop
With the brief stop.
The lamp tan
In a short span.
The Big Shot
In a good spot.
And the brain strain
And the heart pain.
And the cat naps

Till the spring snaps--
And the fun's done!

When we begin to seriously analyze our lives, we see that our problem is not only with sin but with time. We do not have enough time to make all the money we crave. We do not have enough time to go all the places there are to go. We do not have enough time for all the available thrills and excitements that life has to offer. We are trapped for the lack of time, and if we're not careful we will borrow so much today from tomorrow that we will bankrupt our souls before our years are spent.

We are fast becoming spiritual paupers because too much of our time has been dedicated to material priorities. However, because we cannot serve God and mammon and because the fibers of life can only be stretched so far, somehow we must learn to make the most of our time. We must recognize our God-given limitations and find rest for our souls.

Paul, in writing to the Ephesian Christians, encouraged them to be strongly committed to the Christian life. Knowing the immoral character of that pagan city, he enumerated many sins they were to avoid if they were to be imitators of God. He also urged them to walk in the light of their knowledge of Christ. Inserted in the middle of his dissertation is a pungent statement which summarizes life. Paul said, "Make the most of your time because the days are evil."

Not only was this statement pertinent for first-century Christians, it has a wealth of meaning for us today. There are laborers, professionals, and business people all around us, ready to push the panic button because of increased responsibilities. We have teachers facing the growing demands of quality education. We have students caught in the frustrations of the academic runaround. We have housewives trying to cope with a family full of disorientation. We have elderly people who are wondering what in the world has happened to the slower pace of another generation.

It may be well for us all to sit back and relax, take a deep breath, and forget for a few moments those other things which have dominated our attention and energy. It might be well for us to reflect on some things that might help us make the best use of our time.

Of course there is no revised daylight savings plan designed to give us an extra hour of work or play. Although our doctors have already told us to slow down, the prospects of it are very slim. Science and technology have made ours a complex world, and to some extent we are destined to adjust to its complexities.

Our greatest need may be to find a spiritual base from which to operate in this world on the move, where time is the most precious ingredient. Let us consider some ways in which we can adjust to the increasing demands upon our time.

In the first place, if we want to make the most

of our time, we need to stop going around unforgiven. We've got to do something about our sin problem. It's bad enough trying to survive in our competitive, complicated society without having the added burden of unconfessed and unforgiven sins. The writer of Hebrews gives us excellent advice when he says, "Let us throw off every weight of sin that holds on to us so that we may run with determination the race that is before us."

A nagging guilt complex is one of the most devastating and time-consuming struggles of our lives. Young people will never be the students they could be while struggling with a heavy conscience. Adults will never reach their occupational potential until they work with a clear conscience. We cannot be the people God has created us to be as long as the burden of sin, guilt, and inner turmoil is our daily companion.

David had been destined and created by God to be a great king and leader of God's movement for his day. But as the result of his unconfessed and unforgiven sin, he almost lost his charismatic authority. He almost lost his soul. It was not until he came clean with God that he found the strength of character to continue as king and leader of his people. In his honesty he found God as the only source of his recovery.

The prodigal son left his father's house in search of a pleasurable utopia. But to his chagrin, he found no such place. Instead, he was left with a defeated soul that had spent itself in reckless living. Sin which had promised him peace and joy had left him only pain and sorrow. When he came to his senses and made an honest confession, he found the courage to return to his home. He returned to responsible living again.

There is absolutely no way we can survive the rapid pace of modern living without dealing with our sin problem. There is no way we can continue in our sin and make the most of our time. Somehow we must find the courage to come clean with God. We must learn to be honest with ourselves and with others. In the sacredness of that kind of confession, we can realize our great capacities in Christ Jesus.

We simply do not have the time, and it is far too exhausting, to be phony during this brief pit stop we have on this racing world of ours. What a relief it is to know that while we do have to adjust to the fast pace of modern living, we can at least leave our sins with Jesus.

In the second place, if we want to make the most of our time, we must stop going around unforgiving. In this life, not only are we faced with the burden of our own unforgiven sins, too often we are tantalized by the sins of others simply because we refuse to forgive them. Revenge, retaliation, hostility, and criticism are some of the most defeating attitudes of our lives. We might do well to inventory the amount of time we spend in criticizing those who do not conform to our pattern of living or to our way of seeing things. We spend a lot of mental energy in hostility and anger toward those who we think have mistreated us. We do many things and spend much money motivated by a subtle revenge to get even or to get back at someone. All this we do simply because we refuse to forgive. This unforgiving style of life is time-consuming and demoralizing in a day when we need to be at our best.

Jesus was right. If we want to make the most of our time, we must realize this is not "an-eye-for-an-eye-and-a-tooth-for-a-tooth" world. We are not equipped to properly punish one another. If we return evil for evil we will surely be consumed by it. We are much too limited and our own human discrepancies are far too apparent for us to try to play God. Let us resign from the exhausting task of trying to set everybody straight.

Let us learn to forgive those who trespass against us, even as God forgives us of our own trespasses. Let us learn from the grace that has been extended to us to make the same offer to others. Jesus makes it quite clear that only as we forgive others are we able to appropriate divine forgiveness into our own lives. As we develop a forgiving disposition, we are a long way toward making the most of our time.

In the third place, if we want to make the most of our time, we must learn to deal with our distorted sense of values. Because the accumulation of things has dominated so much of our attention and energy, we are on the verge of selling our souls for a mess of pottage. The almighty dollar has become our god, and everything we do must be weighed in terms of its economic value.

No longer is our ambition merely to "keep up with the Joneses," but now it is to be ahead of them. We are on the outs with many of our friends, not because they have mistreated us, but because they have committed the crime of getting ahead of us. Someone gets the promotion a notch or two above us at work, and it devastates us. Our friends build a finer home in a nicer section of town, and it bothers us. Classmates with whom we are competing get better grades, and we cannot stand it. All this happens because of a distorted sense of values.

The economic structures of our society have made us this way. They have pitted us against one another in order to keep selling us things. We have been advertised into moral and financial bankruptcy. We have succumbed to the pressure of appearing to be affluent. We have been gullible to the point of losing ourselves in the attempt to stay ahead and maintain our social prestige. It's an exhausting way to live, but how do we change the pattern until we have changed our sense of values?

Jesus comes to our rescue by saying that a person's life is never ultimately evaluated in terms of his or her possessions. "What shall it profit a man if he gain the whole world and lose his soul?" Jesus calls our attention to the spiritual dimension of life, which takes precedence over and adds meaning to whatever material blessings we receive.

The psalmist also helps us when he reminds us

to "trust in the Lord . . . delight yourself in the Lord and He will give you the desires of your heart." Carlyle Marney has an interesting, perhaps more literal, translation which says, "Trust in the Lord . . . seek your happiness in the Lord, and He will fix your 'wanter.'" Here is, no doubt, the need for our modern dilemma. Many of us need to have our "wanters" fixed because they can easily get out of perspective.

Here we are today, victims of our own fantasies, caught in the web of our own ambitions, and the only cure for our exhaustion is worship. The truth of the matter is if we want to make the most of our time, we have to begin with God. Only God can help us stop going around unforgiven, carrying the weight and worry of our sins upon our souls. Only God can give us a forgiving disposition whereby our time can be better spent than trying to seek revenge. Only God alone can cure our diseased "wanters."

If we want to make the most of our time, then we must let God use us in changing this world that is running rampantly away from us. Paul reminded us in our scripture that these are evil times. We must learn to insert some love where hate has prevailed. We must exert some courage where cowards tend to escape responsible living. We must produce hope where there has been an awesome amount of fear. We must produce peace where there has been pain, joy where there has been sorrow, and forgiveness where there has been sin.

Let us never forget two strong Biblical

observations: "Today is the day of salvation. Now is the accepted time." "Let us not become weary in doing good, for at the proper time we will reap a harvest if we do not give up."

REFLECTION

Life moves on with each beat of the heart, each journey completed, and each goal achieved. The past is memory and the future is hope. There is no way to change the scheme of things. We simply adjust to the patterns of our existence. Life is not so much a matter of altering circumstances as it is a matter of altering attitudes. The passing of time is inevitable. The longer we live, the less likely it is we will live much longer.

The key to happiness is not found in the amount of time lived, but in the quality of time given to things that really matter. Age is relative. Whatever is left of us in terms of time and energy can be productive if we are committed to the best that is within us. God does not hand us life on a silver platter. We are created with a freedom to make the most or the least out of what happens to us.

Time is the stuff life is made of, and it can be

either our enemy or our friend. We have the capacity to make it harmful or helpful. For example, it takes time to become a reprobate. It takes time to become addicted to evil's cunning devices. It takes time to sin away our spiritual birthrights. It takes time to develop a hateful disposition. It takes time to nurture our hates and hostilities. It takes time to make enemies.

On the other hand, however, it takes time to be holy. It takes time to develop our walk with God. It takes time to cultivate a disposition of grace. It takes time to learn the lessons of love and forgiveness. It takes time to do unto others as we would have them do unto us. It takes time to make friends and have a godly influence. It takes time to fulfill our highest hopes. It takes time to be in love with life. It takes time to make time our friend.

The stewardship of time, therefore, is one of life's most demanding requirements. We cannot treat time as though we have an inexhaustible supply. There are precious moments to be guarded and there are difficult times to be endured. There are happy days to celebrate and sorrowful events to mourn. Being good stewards of time means that we learn and grow as we adjust to whatever life imposes upon us. Faith prepares us for the unexpected. Love gives us a new lease on life. Hope anticipates God's glorious tomorrow. Worship enables us to fit the pieces of life's puzzle into the time frame of our allotted days.

Have a happy future with God and with loved ones who help you make the most of your time.

PRAYER

Lord, we come to You today
with time on our minds.
The clock ticks;
the calendar turns;
the seasons come and go.
We wish for more time
and yet we waste much of what we have.
Teach us, O Lord,
how to make the most of every moment.
We recognize You as the Creator
and Lord of time.
We offer You
the praise of our lips,
the songs of our hearts,
the meditations of our minds,
and the labor of our hands.
We ask, O Lord,
that You bless the secular
as well as the sacred
aspects of our lives.
We want to worship You
not only in the sanctuary
but by the way we honor You
in our daily routines.
Thank You for a time to be holy
and a time to be human.
Forgive us when we fail to be both.
Amen.

Chapter 9

THE JOURNEY OF PERSONAL FAITH
II Timothy 1:7-14

The apostle Paul had a special word of personal witness for young Timothy. He wrote, "I know whom I have believed and am persuaded that He is able to keep that which I have committed unto Him against that day." Let the tempo of this text ring in our ears. Let the beauty of its confidence cultivate within us a sense of assurance.

What an optimistic outlook for a man most likely in prison because of his faith! Such a statement makes us ashamed of our negative attitudes toward church, toward life, and toward religion. We find ourselves almost envious of a person with such a godly grasp of real religion. In this expression of his faith, Paul is certain and unhesitating. He seems so sure that God is in control of his circumstances.

We wish similar words could flow from our lips with the same relaxed assurance. But we are often so doubtful, so hesitant, and so tentative in our loyalty and devotion. We find ourselves asking, "How can Paul be so sure? What makes him so different from us? Is it really possible for us to be affected by a similar confidence?"

For these very legitimate questions, let us

consider three areas of thought. Let us look at why Paul's religion was real. Let us explore why our own religion is not as real as we would like it to be. Finally, let us pursue what we can do about it.

In the first place, why *was* Paul's religion real? How do we explain the depth of his certainty?

Paul was a man who, in the realm of faith, had made a personal discovery. Paul's experience was not based on hearsay. These words to Timothy are not the echo of rumors blown around during that first century. They are the result of many personal, soul-shaking events for Paul. They represent the spiritual shock of a blinding flash on that Damascus road where the Lord Christ became a real partner in Paul's life.

These words to young Timothy reflect the careful supervision and teaching of early church leaders during Paul's initial days as a Christian. They reveal the kind of personal faith that launched him on his missionary journeys. These words form the personal testimony of a man who had been with Jesus and found Him more than adequate to meet all the circumstances of his life.

Paul's religion was real because it was his own. It was wrought in the texture of his own life and thought. It had passed through the fires of his own soul. He was not mechanically repeating what he had heard someone else say. His words were warmed by the coals from the altar of his own personal dedication. Notice how freshly Paul's personal pronouns leap out at us. He wrote, "*I* know," "*I* believe," "*I* am persuaded," "that which *I* have committed unto Him against that day."

How needful this is for all of us! Our experience cannot be the carbon copy of some pastor, some religious celebrity, some Sunday School teacher, or some Christian friend. Somewhere in the closet of our own personal lives, we must work out our own salvation with fear and trembling. We can never, never experience the experience of others.

Jesus accented this fact in His comments to Nicodemus when He insisted, "You must be born again." Just as every person must have an individual and personal *natural* birth, so must every person have an individual and personal *spiritual* birth.

We are not part of God's kingdom simply because we are well-born. We cannot live like spiritual parasites off the faith of our fathers. If our religion is going to be real, it will develop on our journey toward a personal faith.

Paul's religion was real because he was constantly aware of God's forgiveness through Jesus Christ. As we read his spiritually affluent letters, we know that Paul daily reminded himself of his own worthlessness and accented the greatness of God's grace. Acts 26 records one of Paul's last opportunities to give testimony of his faith before government authorities. As he stood before Agrippa he reviewed the circumstances of his life. He gave special attention to God's grace in forgiving him and calling him to be a minister to the Gentiles.

Nothing can be more stimulating to our faith than to daily confront the reality of God's forgiveness. David bore testimony to the strength of forgiveness as he wrote in Psalm 32, "Blessed is he whose transgression is forgiven, whose sin is covered. Blessed is the man to whom the Lord imputes no iniquity, and in whose spirit there is no guile."

Paul's religion was real because he experienced divine power. It prompted him to say, "I can do all things through Christ who strengthens me." Paul felt that power as he battled the forces of sin in every pagan city and as he confronted the Judaizers in every synagogue. As he opposed emperor worship in every capital and as he wrestled with the powers and principalities of evil everywhere, Paul was aware of God's guiding presence. Such assurance is indeed "the victory that overcomes the world."

Paul's religion was real because it produced within him a Christian disposition. The real test of a religious experience is what it makes of us. What kind of spirit is within us? What godly attitudes are established?

For some, religion is nothing but an ego trip or a forum for debate. It is a reason to look down on others. Church for these folk becomes more of an occasion to dispense anger than to share love.

What is religion doing to you? It produced in Paul a dynamic Christian personality. Real religion will do it every time.

To review the genuineness of Paul's faith leaves

us with the struggle to know why ours is often so limited and unproductive. Do you think sometimes we are guilty of professing a faith we do not have in order to create a faith we want? Do we *talk* more faith than we *do*? Are we whistling in the dark, when in reality the dark has consumed us? When all is said and done, is there usually more said than done?

We want to believe in God; yet, somehow our fickle faith is plagued by doubt. We are terribly suspicious of things that look too supernatural. Sometimes it seems as though we are actually embarrassed to acknowledge the input God has in our lives. We often refuse to confess a faith experience which we think others might find difficult to believe.

What has happened to the faith of our fathers? Where is that spiritual heritage handed down to us by the blood, sweat, and tears of our forebears?

We come to worship, but we have little or no communion with God. We come to sing, but seldom do the melody and the music of an inner joy find expression. We come to study, but the Spirit of the Master Teacher never seems to penetrate the outer shell of our superficial commitments.

We come to pray, but we often echo the prayer patterns of a past generation, and nothing fresh and vital ever seems to issue forth in our conversations with God. Does not God sometimes get tired of hearing the same cliches, the same God-talk, and the same artificial rhetoric?

We come to preach, but often our sermons

113

become little more than dramatic productions. It's because people would much rather be entertained than inspired and challenged by the Word of God.

A terrible heresy of our time is that everything has to be scaled down to our understanding. We dream of so much and settle for so little. The preacher does not go deeply into the scriptures or any of life's issues for fear he will lose the greater portion of his congregation. He skims the surface of superficial piety and deals with sentimental niceties so that folk will praise him as being their kind of preacher. All the time he is robbing them of the prophetic voice they need to hear. Perhaps the sermon is losing its place in worship and will be replaced by little choruses and emotionally stimulating exercises. Someone has given these critiques of preaching: "What did he preach about? I don't know. He never said." "He shot a sermon in the air. It fell to earth; I know not where." "His weekly drawl, though short, was much too long." "The sermon is too long. Cut it in half; either half will do."

We call ourselves Christians, and yet the conditions of our world and community are not greatly affected by that fact. The prophet Amos dealt with a similar situation centuries ago. Note what he hears the Lord saying to the worshipers of his day in Amos 5:21-24: "I hate, I despise your feasts, and I take no delight in your solemn assemblies. . . . Take away from me the noise of your songs. To the melody of your harps I will not listen. But let justice roll down like waters, and righteousness like a mighty stream."

Consider a modern paraphrase of this passage: "I hate your Christmas celebrations and your Easter festivities. I will take no delight in your superficial Sunday services. Your preaching is nothing more than oratorical display. Your singing has been reduced to theatrical performance. Your teaching is artificial and insincere. In your giving you have become hypocritical stewards, and as listeners you have become sarcastic critics. Let your compassion and your fair-mindedness roll down like waters over the Norris Dam, and let your right living flow like the floodwaters of the Tennessee River."

Here we see a word for our day. We have focused upon the routine of religious activity and lost our closeness to God. We have been so busy doing things in the name of God, we haven't taken time to know God.

What, then, can we do to renew our personal journey with God? Most of us, and maybe all of us, need to give ourselves to God. Oh, we believe in Him. Most of us have made our public professions. But we have not thoroughly committed ourselves to Him. We have not really given God a chance in our lives.

We spend sixteen hours of the day thinking about the things of the world and perhaps, at most, five minutes remembering our Creator. No wonder our faith is feeble. It is impossible to be worldly minded six days a week and expect to be spiritually minded for one hour on Sunday. It is impossible to be selfish,

115

superficial, and cynical on our feet, and then on our knees become something else.

A friend once said, "If we are never alone with God, it is not because we are too busy. It is because we do not wish to be alone with Him. It is too painful." Perhaps we do not want His companionship, but, oh, how we need it!

One of our greatest needs is to commit ourselves to the journey of becoming growing, invigorating, and exciting participants in everything God wants us to experience. Sometimes when we have a good experience with God, we want to settle down with it and enshrine it. We even idolize it, so that it keeps us from going on to other experiences God wishes us to have.

God is not static. God is not always in the same place and in the same experiences. God is out there on the edge of our being, drawing us on and meeting us in new experiences. He is trying to deepen our understanding of faith as we make the journey with Him. The Bible tells us the greatest sin of all is frustrating the Holy Spirit. Basically that means not making the spiritual journey. It means not looking for God in every event of our lives and not yielding to Him a hundred times a day as we grow and develop in the life of faith.

No, we're not there yet; none of us are. To understand this, the words of the poet Robert Frost come to mind: "We have promises to keep, and miles to go before we sleep, and miles to go before we sleep."

Another thing we need is to clean up our lives and become fit vessels for the dwelling of God's Spirit. The reason God is not real is not because He is an elusive person. The contrary is true, because it is God who is seeking us. The fact is our sinful lives will not grant Him entrance.

The story is told of a pastor who was dealing with a young intellect in his church. He appeared to be a fine young man, but was always doubting the great truths of the faith. Often the pastor would counsel him on basic religious matters which the fellow had difficulty accepting. Finally one day, almost in desperation, the pastor asked, "Young man, are you having trouble with the Ten Commandments?" After a long hesitation, the young man broke. He began to share bits of his life and eventually confessed that his real problem was moral.

Perhaps for many of us this is where God needs to become real. He needs to become real in the cleaning process. Listen to the message of the poem written by Barbara J. Thompson entitled "Spring Cleaning":

> God knocked at the door of my heart one day
> And I looked for a place to hide.
> My soul was cluttered and choked with debris
> And things were untidy inside.
> I needed some time to put matters right,
> Surprised He would call on me.

My soul needed cleaning from bottom to top;
There were things He should not see.
There were tasks neglected, long overdue,
Cobwebs to be brushed from the wall,
Rugs to be shaken, windows cleaned up.
I had not expected His call.
I stood with my hand on the latch of the door
And gazed at the mess in the room.
When I opened the door, my soul blushed to see
God had left on my doorstep a broom.

The question emerges again. Are we on this journey of personal faith? What if the morning dawn should find us on our knees in prayer? What if the noonday heat should bathe our brows with the sweat of honest toil? What if the sunset breeze should whisper God's "well done" for a day lived in the context of His will? What if the dark of night should bring the peaceful sleep of a clear conscience?

It's a very simple philosophy of life that keeps us close to the source of happiness and contentment. Life does not have to be complicated and busy to have meaning and power. Jesus does not call us to be spiritual computers with answers and printouts on every issue. He simply calls us to do His will, and in that surrender, we discover life's deepest treasures.

What if there is a God and He is with us right now? Would that not be too wonderful for words? Remember, "we have promises to keep, and miles to go before we sleep, and miles to go before we sleep."

REFLECTION

A recent extended illness and doctor-imposed exile created several limitations which required a certain amount of adjustment for me. It was not easy being still when in the past I was so much on the go. It was not easy avoiding people when people had been my profession. It was not easy depending on others for yard work, gardening, and outside chores which were once my enjoyable pastime. It was not easy being away from folk who for seventeen and one-half years had been family to me. It was not easy adjusting to the fact that I had an illness that limited my lifestyle.

None of these and other limitations were easy, but they were necessary. No doubt, acceptance was part of the healing process. In fact, there were spiritual benefits to such confinement. The Apostle Paul and I became reacquainted. I began reading him not from the standpoint of sermon preparation, but for revelation into his inner being. I tried to grasp the heartbeat of this pivotal New Testament character. Rather than pick selected verses and take them out of context, I strove to see the total thrust of Paul's writings. I looked at his confessed humanity and inconsistencies. I was impressed with his sense of divine inspiration which motivated his ministry and his writing. I liked how he sometimes paused to say, "This is my own opinion." Then again, he gave God credit for his thoughts. His candor, humility and love give his letters a sense of authenticity and genuine

119

understanding of life's struggles.

Another serendipity of my confinement was the sense of stillness which contributes to a consciousness of God. In this God-kind of quietness, prayer becomes so much more than the recitation of words. It is the awe of feeling God's presence which sometimes the noise of speaking interrupts. Even though this period of rest required many adjustments, I am convinced there is a silence about life that promotes both spiritual and physical healing. May it be so for you in your daily transactions.

PRAYER

Where were You, Lord,
when the lights went out of my life?
When that dear one left me,
I felt as though the heavens had forsaken me
and nothing but earth
was bearing the burden of my bones.
Where were You, Lord,
when the tempter overtook me?

I felt as if the angels
were pointing their fingers of scorn at me
and I had no other recourse
than to hide in the shadows of iniquity.
Where were You, Lord,
when my friends forsook me?
I assumed You were in on the plot
and I lashed out at Your church
as well as other people.
Where were You, Lord,
when sickness came?
I cursed the author of disease
as I pampered myself
with thoughts of dying.
Where were You, Lord,
when my finances crumbled?
I blamed You for making me tithe
and not letting me mourn for my mammon.
When despair, O Lord, was my daily diet,
I developed indigestion of the soul
because I ignored the Bread of Life.
When religious drought
had parched every aspect of my being,
there was no melody to sing
about the "showers of blessings."
I come to You, O God,
in hopes of finding my way.
Thank You for waiting to light up my life
with the torch of Your love.
Thank You for helping me

121

to break down and call for Your help.
You have taught me much
through life's adversities.
May the lessons of my life
and the words of my mouth
bless others on their journey.
Amen.

Chapter 10

A NEW KIND OF HONESTY

Matthew 23:1-12

A certain man had been the object of concern for the church for several years. He was not necessarily a bad man; he just didn't attend church and had never made a profession of faith. His wife, family members, and a host of neighbors would often talk with him about his need to be a Christian and to join the church.

To everyone's surprise, one Sunday he was in church, and when the invitation was given he came forward with a request to tell his story. He told a stirring story about a vision he had at his barn. He described how a great ball of light came down from heaven and touched him. He explained how the barn was aglow with the presence of this tremendous light. He also expressed his desire to join the church. A deacon made the motion that they accept him, and the church voted him in.

On the way home his wife chastised him greatly for making up such a tale as that. She exclaimed, "We don't even have a barn, and when did you have such a vision as this?" All week long she scolded him for his concocted story of conversion.

The next Sunday morning the man was in

church again, came forward during the invitation, and asked to express himself. He explained how he had lied about having a vision simply because he thought that was what you had to do to join the church. The same man who made a motion to take him in made another motion that they kick him out.

On the way home that day the man told his wife, "You know, Honey, church is a funny thing."

"How is that?" she questioned.

He said, "Well, they took me in for lying, and then kicked me out when I was telling the truth."

The gospels lead us to believe that the most repulsive sins to Jesus were pretension and hypocrisy. It was the basic dishonesty of the scribes and Pharisees that drew the most severe criticism from the Master. He could dine with an inquisitive tax collector who was noted for his legal thievery. He could become a close associate of a reformed harlot named Mary Magdalene. He could encourage an embarrassed adulteress to go and sin no more. He could offer the paradise of God to a repentant thief on the cross. But to the Pharisee who pretended to be something he was not, Jesus had nothing but scalding words of rebuke.

This is not to say that Jesus condoned the sins of robbery, adultery, and murder. It simply illustrates that Jesus found more in common with the honest sinners, the so-called moral reprobates of his day, than with the dishonest and pretentious keepers of the law. Jesus had problems with people who could judge everyone else but saw no inconsistency in their own behavior.

Jesus spent a great deal of His ministry denouncing the Pharisees because He could see beneath the surface of their superficial piety. He saw the real persons they were, and there He found all the sins common to humankind. But they were unwilling to admit them. They would not confess their sins, but tried to hide them behind a cloak of religious display. Jesus could not tolerate this hypocrisy because He knew that the way to salvation was dependent on an honest evaluation of oneself before God and man.

Jesus found it impossible to deal with people who had allowed their religion to harden into self-righteousness. Therefore, the major thrust of His preaching and counseling was an appeal for a new kind of honesty. It was an honesty that would sweep away the sham, pretense, and artificial masks of hypocrisy. It was the kind of honesty that would enable people to bear their souls to God and deal honestly with others.

Jesus helped numerous folk face the reality of their own situations, and in so doing they found redemption. In His confrontation with Nicodemus, Jesus was able to get him to see that all the prestige his religious system had given him was not adequate to deal with his inner needs. Even though he was a ruler of the Jews, there was something lacking in the life of Nicodemus. In that moment of rare honesty, Jesus helped him realize that his greatest need was rebirth.

When Jesus encountered the rich young ruler with his inquiry about eternal life, He found a commendable collection of good deeds by the young man. However, when Jesus pulled aside the mask and put His finger on the nerve of the young man's life, He found that money was his god. His religion was a front. The real commitment of his life was to his possessions, and he went away sorrowfully.

As Jesus sat on the rim of Jacob's well talking to a Samaritan woman of ill repute, He was able to work behind her dishonest barriers of defense. He enabled her to see herself as she really was, and in the context of that honest encounter with herself and with the Christ, something happened. Something happened which caused her to hasten into the city, inviting other people to come and see the Messiah. As a result of her testimony, many came and believed.

Jesus, in His preaching and teaching, insisted on "telling it like it is." Some could not measure up to that kind of truth and followed Him no more. Others became openly hostile toward Him and sought to destroy Him. Yet many others found redemption in this new kind of honesty.

A great need of our day is to recapture the kind of honesty that Jesus instilled in those early followers. It was a kind of honesty that gave them mental, emotional, and spiritual stability amid the turmoil of their lives.

No doubt, a major factor leading to emotional and mental breakdown today is the fact that we have deceived and have been deceived so much, and we have lived in a world of hypocrisy so long, we have lost the meaning of life and spiritually are out of touch with reality. Our day is sadly characterized by pretense and insincerity. There seems to be no one we can really trust. We find ourselves searching for a person who is genuine, who is honest, who is authentic, who is real. And yet we find ourselves so deficient in these same qualities. In our discouragement we cry with Jeremiah, "The heart is deceitful above all things and desperately wicked; who can understand it?"

Our day has become seriously infected by a loss of integrity. Because of political maneuvering and questionable activities by public officials, many people are losing confidence in the integrity of our government. Because of shady business deals, price-fixing, and deceitful practices of salesmanship, many people are losing confidence in the integrity of our business world. Because of inaccuracies and the slanting of news articles, most folk are losing confidence in the integrity of the news media. Because of the broadening gap that exists between what Christians preach and what they practice, there are serious doubts concerning the integrity of the church.

The sad part of this commentary on our times is that in one way or another we all contribute to this dilemma. The sham, the pretense, and the dishonesty of our times are the result of the inevitable hypocrite that is in each of us. When Jesus verbally chastised the Pharisees, we feel the same rebuke because of our own personal hypocrisy.

Let us, therefore, look at how we contribute to the hypocrisy of our times. There are two ways in

127

which we tend to be hypocritical--first of all, by pretending to be better than we are; secondly, by pretending to be worse than we really are. Let us explore these two hypocritical approaches.

In the first place, we contribute to the hypocrisy of our times by pretending to be better than we are. Much of this happens in the church and with church people, just like it did in the days of Jesus. We begin it all by training our children to always look happy and successful and never share their true feelings in public.

Keith Miller tells of a little girl who was playing on the floor of a large department store. A big man came along and accidently stepped on her hand. She immediately began to scream loudly from the pain. Everyone turned to look. The mother jerked the little girl up from the floor in embarrassment and said, "Sh, sh! Don't cry here in front of all these people." Miller said he would always remember the confused look on the little girl's face as she stared at her throbbing, swollen hand, wondering why she could not cry.

Because we have been trained well at pretense as children, when we are grown we become rather successful in putting forth the image expected of us in every situation. As a result, our churches are filled with people who outwardly look contented and at peace. Inwardly, however, they are confused, guilty, and frightened and want desperately for someone to love them.

Let me illustrate what I mean by the pretense of being better than we are. Consider a typical family on a given Sunday morning getting ready for church. On this particular morning everyone was cross and fussy. The mother was mad at the father. The father was mad at his wife. The children were fussing at one another and angered their parents greatly. Anger and hatred prevailed in that household because no one was willing to repent or forgive.

On the way to church the car literally vibrated with statements of anger, confusion, and family chaos. But when they got out of the car after arriving at church, everyone put on their Sunday smiles. In Sunday School Mrs. Church Member was called on to pray in her class, so she changed into her sweet tone and prayed a beautiful but mechanical prayer thanking God for the home and the family. As she sat down everyone was thinking, "My, what a wonderful Christian mother and wife she must be!"

Mr. Church Member taught a great Sunday School lesson, and, of all things, it was on love and family relations. After he had finished, his class members thought he must be an ideal father and husband.

As the family went into worship after meeting at their appointed places, they were still all smiles, except for an occasional "dagger" look at one another. However, they all joined in vigorously and sang "Oh, How I Love Jesus." As the sermon was preached and the invitation was given, each of them felt a need to confess their sins and recommit their lives. But they refused to go forward for fear the folk of the church would think they were having trouble in their home.

Do you see how easily we pretend to be better than we are? A person once told me he wanted to come forward after my sermon and rededicate his life, but he was afraid someone would think he had done something bad. Well, we have all done something bad. "All have sinned and come short of the glory of God."

Isn't it a sad commentary on a church when a person cannot find the courage to confess his need before such a self-sufficient looking group? This happens when we pretend to be better than we are. Our world will never be seriously affected by the church as long as Christians insist on flexing their spiritual muscles and looking down their noses at the rest of the world. The fact that we are church members doesn't ever mean we are any better than anyone else. I hope it does mean that we are trying harder. Therefore, if we will all stop pretending, we can help one another confess our need of Christ.

On the other hand, we contribute to the hypocrisy of our day by pretending to be worse than we really are. We live in a highly technological and scientific world where religious faith for some is obsolete and unpopular. Many folk, especially youth, try to appear more secular and sinful than they really are. To them it seems to be a mark of intellectual distinction to doubt God and question religion. But underneath their pretense they really believe and know better.

Some people have overreacted to the hypocrisy

of pretending to be more than what they are and have become another kind of hypocrite. It is the hypocrisy of pretending to be worse than what they are. Jesus had something to say to this kind of hypocrisy also. He said, "Men do not light a candle and put it under a bushel, but on a candlestick, and it gives light to all who are in the house. Let your light so shine before men, that they may see your good works and glorify your Father in heaven."

So you see, to have light and refuse to set it out is another kind of hypocrisy. If you are honest, then you are a hypocrite if you do not appear honest. If you are morally decent, you are a hypocrite if you do not appear decent. If you believe in God, then you are a hypocrite if you fail to show faith in Him. If you have character, then you are a hypocrite if you are careless with your reputation. We must commit ourselves to the best we know and then try by God's help to live up to it.

A noted preacher was speaking to a group of Harvard students some years ago, and he challenged them with this thought: "Ladies and gentlemen, in this sophisticated day of learning, seem as Christian as you really are!" Some hypocrites need to be told, "Be as good as you seem." Other hypocrites need to be told, "Seem as good as you are."

What is the answer to the hypocrisy of our day? I think it is a new kind of honesty that recognizes and faces squarely the nature and the extent of our deceitfulness with God, with each other, and with ourselves. Honesty may not be the front door to the kingdom of God, but it is the latchstring to every door in His house.

This kind of honesty is the ability to level with God. In the spirit of this honesty we no longer feel compelled to camouflage our real selves in fancy-sounding prayers using worn out cliches. We simply confess our sins, admit our weaknesses, and seek the help of God. In the freedom of this kind of honesty we are able to talk to God about our hatred and resentments, our lusts and our pride, and our selfishness and greed, and in so doing, we find forgiveness and strength.

Let me hasten to say that this kind of honesty does not mean we are free from these evils in our lives. But it does mean that we are free from pretending they are not there. In the spirit of this kind of honesty we no longer feel compelled to impress our friends with our goodness. We are free to be ourselves and to be loved and accepted for who we are and who we can be by the grace of God.

This does not mean everyone will like us. It does mean, however, we will no longer feel the need to pretend or show off in order to be accepted and loved. We will no longer have to worry what people might think if we should make a public commitment of our lives to Christ. We are free from the restricting power of pretense. We are free to be God's person, and, oh, what a relief that is!

Betty was a young, attractive mother of three

small children, but her marriage was on the rocks. She was a party-type girl who wore provocative clothes and told shocking stories in mixed company. She had not been to church for years, but one day, out of her deep need, she came and gave herself as honestly as she knew how to Christ her Savior.

Her life changed in a meaningful way. Eight weeks later she had this to say to a church group which had met for prayer: "You know, all my life I've been trying to get your attention. I showed off, I told dirty stories, and I did all kinds of things to get you to notice me and to love me. And when you didn't," she said, "I gossiped about you--cut you to ribbons behind your backs--because I was miserable. I wanted to be something. I wanted so much to be something in your eyes. But now," she said with deep emotion, "for the first time in my life I'm happy to be 'nothing' for Jesus Christ. I'm happy to be just the mother of my children and the wife of Joe." Betty no longer had to pretend or show off. She was free by God's help to be herself.

Come into the healing and redeeming realm of honesty. An honesty which God honors. An honesty which simply professes, "Nothing in my hands I bring; simply to Thy cross I cling."

Be done with pretense. God will honor your sincerity.

REFLECTION

The hummingbird is yet another parable of my backyard creatures. He is a nervous little critter who buzzes in for a sip of nectar from red flowers or sugar water from the red feeder. He is rather antisocial in his behavior. He gets a quick drink and off he goes. I worry about his digestion. Does nectar soothe his busy stomach?

He never lingers long enough for me to get a good look at him. It is as though he tries to hide himself in a blur of busy wings and rapid movement. Does he ever sleep, I wonder, or does he ever slow down enough to communicate with other birds? When on rare occasions he hesitates, he is a beautiful, petite creature with an impressive red ring around his neck. Yet after one quick glance, his beauty is lost amid the flurry of his feathery activity. I would like to get to know my tiny friend, but he seems too busy for human acquaintance.

The hummingbird reminds me of some people, perhaps myself at times. We hurry around in such a maze of activity we hardly pause to smell the flowers from which we draw sweetness. We flutter in flight as we escape those who would cause us to have serious thoughts about ourselves. It is a subtle disguise in which we camouflage our true feelings. We know no one and no one knows us, because we never stop long enough to get acquainted.

Being involved in a lot of things sometimes

protects us from having to do a few things well. We never expose the beauty of our personalities nor the depth of our thoughts. Like the hummingbird, we buzz off before anyone can see us as we are. Such a hurried and busy approach to life is fine for the hummingbird because it is his nature. We humans, however, are not equipped for such a rapid pace. We are created with a need for stillness, meditation, and worship. If we try to imitate the hummingbird, we'll wear out our wings before our years are spent.

PRAYER

Thank You, Lord,
for the purity of Your purpose,
the honesty of Your appeal,
and the integrity of Your grace.
We are blessed by Your consistency.
We find peace in Your dependability.
Your never-changing truth
is a light unto our paths.

135

Help us, O Lord,
to be authentic people.
We confess our pretense.
We want to be genuine
in the expression of our faith,
but often we are hypocritical.
We want to be authentic,
but often we are weak.
We express that which is expected
rather than that which we feel.
We wear so many masks
trying to hide our true identity from others
and even at times from You, O Lord.
We confuse ourselves, Lord,
and at times we are not sure
we even know who we are.
Forgive us, Lord, for the insincerities
which creep into the daily practice of our faith.
Give us the courage, Lord,
to admit who we are
and to begin at that point
to grow in Your grace.
Amen.

Chapter 11

LOVE THAT BINDS

Psalm 55:4-8; Jeremiah 9:2; Matthew 26:39

David, the great king of Israel, is pacing back and forth across the roof of his palace. He is nervous and restless; uneasiness shows in his face. His mind is weary and worn with the problems of government. His heart is heavy with grief and despair. His beloved country is torn with civil war and strife. His own son is leading the insurrection. What can he do? What can he do? He wrings his hands in absolute helplessness.

Suddenly a dove perches on the ledge of the palace roof. David moves as if to stroke its feathery form, but it flits off into the peaceful sky. David watches as it makes its carefree journey into the distant somewhere. David's eyes swell with tears of eyestrain as well as heartache, and he mutters to himself, "Oh, that I had the wings of a dove! For then would I fly away and be at rest."

What is wrong with David? This doesn't sound like the same man who wrote, "The Lord is my shepherd; I shall not want." Is this the same person who said, "What time I am afraid I will trust in Thee"? What is wrong with him?

David wanted to escape the pain of a bad situation. He wanted to be free of life's burden for a while. We find ourselves wanting to say, "But, David, you can't run away. You are the king. You are the sweet singer of Israel. You are a man after God's own heart. You are the most famous ancestor of our Lord."

We are on the verge of being disappointed with David, but then we turn to the book of Jeremiah and read of another who faced a life of pain. Jeremiah had the assignment of living in the latter days of Judah's existence as a nation. He tried to be a voice for God, but he faced harassment, persecution, and even death from his own people. Nothing he said or did seemed to turn his people from the path of destruction on which they were determined to walk. The more he tried to warn, the more it seemed they resented him.

Jeremiah grew weary with people, and in a moment of despair and exhaustion he cried, "Oh, that I had in the wilderness a lodging place for wayfaring men that I might leave my people and go from them." Like David, Jeremiah also wanted to escape. He wanted to be done with people. He wanted to be alone with his thoughts and with his God.

Lest we become disillusioned with these two heroes of the Old Testament, let me hasten to say they are not the only ones who have ever wanted to escape life's difficult assignment. In fact, we turn to the New Testament, and there in Gethsemane we see the lonely form of the Lord Himself bent in prayer.

This session with the Father, however, is not necessarily the sweet communion of quiet meditation. Jesus is in agony. He is struggling in prayer. So great is His anguish that His sweat is like great drops of blood. Out of the trauma of those desperate moments of facing the cross, we hear these words: "Father, if it be Thy will, let this cup pass." Yes, in that moment the Lord Himself wanted to escape. The prospects of rejection, pain, and death overwhelmed His humanity and He cried for relief.

The need to run away at times is in all of us. It's a human tendency to cry for a more pleasant task or an easier assignment. Yet, that is not what life is all about. Deep down, David knew he could not fly away like a dove. Do you know why? Because there was a love that bound him to his task. He was called of God to be the king. He could not sin away his divine obligation. He belonged to something bigger than his own frustration. David had a marvelous capacity to survive his grief and get right with God because of the love that bound him to spiritual reality.

Jeremiah knew there was no lodge in the wilderness where he could escape the pain of people. And do you know why? Because there was a love that bound him to his ministry of tears. The Lord God had placed a message on his lips, and it was a fire within his bones. There was a love that bound him to God's eternal purpose, and he could not escape the increasing burden of its proclamation.

Jesus knew the cup could not pass. It was predetermined that He drink it. For that reason He came into the world. There was a love that bound Him to the Father's will. He was the Word of God made flesh.   He could not escape the trauma of God's ultimate sacrifice.   He was committed to the task of being Lord of lords and King of kings forever and ever, which the cup of His sacrifice made possible.   There was a love that bound Him to the process of salvation, and we praise Him for it.

Do you see what these men are saying to us? If we take this life seriously, if we honor the image of God within us, then there is a love that binds us to the things of God.   There is a love that binds us to all that is decent, honorable, and redemptive about life.   There is a love that binds us to one another and to the life, liberty, and happiness which is everyone's dream.   Let us apply this truth to three great institutions of life--the home, the country, and the church.

In the first place, there is a love that binds us to our homes.   We are bound to the success and survival of the home.   We cannot escape our responsibility to it. We cannot fly away to another nest.   This cup of sacrifice and devotion to our homes is ours to drink.

There are many problems and temptations that face the home today.   Marriage and family are under heavy attack in our permissive and promiscuous society.   It's no easy task to be family amid the economic and social strife of our day.

How many fathers do you know who are facing the financial strain of trying to keep the wolf from the door? They awaken one day to the fact that the wolf had pups, and now they want to fly away.

How many mothers do you know who are facing

a whole family full of disorientation? They are on the verge of nervous exhaustion. They long for that lodging place in the wilderness to get away from it all.

How many children do you know who are anxious to grow older? They want to get away from home as soon as possible. They want to escape to somewhere they think fairy-tale dreams come true.

How many husbands do you know who have had their male egos tickled by some "young thing"? They think this someone understands them, so they are refusing to drink the cup of marital fidelity.

How many wives do you know who are still looking for that storybook romance? They are wondering why their dollhouse fantasies have not come true. In disappointment, they are refusing to drink the cup of marital contentment.

On and on we could go, because there are a lot of seemingly good reasons for us to throw up our hands and run away from our homes. But we cannot! There is a love that binds us to our homes and to those with whom we share this family fellowship. There is a love that binds us to the marriage vows and all the promises we have made to keep the home fires burning.

No, it will not always be easy. But we must drink the cup of personal commitment to the family that time and circumstances and God have given us. Could we not say with confidence that he who would lose his life for his family will save his life and his family? There is a tie that binds us to our home, and that tie is love.

In the second place, there is a love that binds us to our country. When Jesus said, "Render unto Caesar the things that are Caesar's," He gave us a strong reason to be committed to our country. When Paul told us to be subject to the powers of government because they are ordained of God, he described the love that binds us to the things that can make our country strong. For you see, in a country like ours was designed to be, the most patriotic thing you and I can do is to obey the Ten Commandments and follow the Sermon on the Mount. There is a cup of sacrifice that we all must drink if we are to maintain life, liberty, and happiness for all Americans.

We cannot escape the demands of a godly citizenry if "one nation under God" is really our goal. David could not fly away because his nation needed his leadership. His call from God was to control the chaos so that the people of Israel could truly be the people of God. Jeremiah could not retreat to the wilderness. His pulpit was in the city. It was there a faithless nation was losing its ability to survive.

You and I cannot avoid the fact that God has a will for our nation. If you and I belong to Him, then we are bound to the things that can help God realize His dream. Therefore, "God Bless America" is not just a neat song to sing on flag-waving days. It is a prayer that ought to be on the lips of every believing American. There is a tie that binds us to our country. It is the tie of love. For you see, in God we trust, and only in God are we trustworthy.

In the third place, there is a love that binds us to our church. We are committed to its survival. Of course, it's not always easy being church. There is a lot of pain in this body of Christ. Sometimes we get hurt, ridiculed, and even neglected in this fickle fellowship.

Sometimes we try to run away from the awesome assignments that church puts upon us. Sometimes we fuss if too much is said about money. We complain that we are too old to visit, too young to take ministry seriously. We avoid commitment by being against anything new. And we find our biggest escape route in saying "they" run the church. In a thousand different ways we refuse to drink the cup of personal discipleship.

But we cannot run away. If you and I belong to Jesus Christ there is a tie that binds us to His church. We are bound to this gospel of grace and this ministry of faith. We are bound to this fellowship of love and all that it means to be church. There is a tie that binds us to Jesus as the head of the church and Lord of all things. In His Spirit the church lives and moves and has its being.

When Jesus is Lord, there is a tie that binds us to one another. We truly become brothers and sisters in Christ instead of a quarreling congregation that has lost its ability to disagree in love. We no longer feud about who knows the most or who is greatest in the eyes of God. We are bound to things that are more

143

important than our own sagging egos.

There is an ancient legend of two knights who were traveling alone one night, when suddenly they came upon one another by surprise. Their first inclination was to fight, which they did. Long and hard they fought until one of the knights overpowered and killed his opponent. After the conflict the victorious knight got off his horse and removed the helmet of the dead knight. He discovered to his dismay that he had killed his own blood brother. In the darkness he had mistaken his brother for the enemy.

What a parable! When Jesus is Lord, there is enough light to see that our brother is not the enemy. In fact, there is enough love to see that even the enemy is not our enemy. We belong to something more important than trying to make enemies out of anyone who might see the Christian life from another perspective. There is a tie that binds us to our church and to one another. That tie is love. We are brothers and sisters in Christ.

What is this tie that binds us to our homes, our country, and our church? It is a love that will not let us go until we have found peace in His perfect will. It is a pain that will not go away until we are committed to the things of God. It is a hope that in Christ all things become new and renewed, even in our homes, our country, and our church.

Is there a loving tie that binds you to the things of God? If not, then allow Jesus to strengthen the ties of your commitment.

REFLECTION

There is nothing more helpful to our human well-being than relationships which are lasting and loving. People who accept us and care for us contribute greatly to our productivity. These folk form the basis of our support systems, even as we contribute to theirs. As we express a caring disposition toward others, we find fulfillment in the fellowship of love.

In many ways, life is lived at its best when there is a sense of covenant. This means that there are unwritten and subtle agreements we make with those who share some part of our lives. Family is a covenant in which each member is required to make a wholesome contribution to the dynamics of living together. Marriage is a covenant in which fidelity and trust are necessary for its survival. Friendship is a covenant in which common interests and compatible personalities form a network of folk toward whom we have a sense of belonging. Church membership is a covenant in which we are committed to all the things that make us the body of Christ and a fellowship of believers. Work is a covenant in which employer and employee find ways to be mutually beneficial. Country is a covenant in which our accumulated patriotism contributes to a wholesome citizenry.

Life is a series of many covenant relationships and is sorely sabotaged when commitments are not kept. Living in covenant requires a lot of apology, forgiveness, and grace. We are not equipped to find happiness in an atmosphere of hostility. To keep our relationships vital and positive we must control our tendencies toward jealousy, revenge, and misunderstanding. We cannot function amid the tension of broken relationships, nor can we succeed when no one appreciates our efforts.

We have been created by God to live in community where good relationships are vital to our total health. Even when we are prone to hurt someone else, we end up hurting ourselves because ill will is a part of our own self-destruction. We cannot escape the fact that we are in covenant with those who share some part of our lives. Let us not neglect to love even as we have been loved by God.

PRAYER

*Thank You, Lord,
for giving us a love
that binds us to the things that really matter.
Thank You
for helping us focus our affection on You.
We could not love You*

unless You had first loved us.
Our love for others as well as ourselves
is a product of Your redemptive influence.
Give us a strength
to fulfill our commitments.
Help our homes
to be havens of restoration.
May parental love
be rewarded by children's respect.
May husbands and wives
know the power of marital grace.
Give single parents
a love that binds them to their offspring.
Thank You for the tie that binds us together
in the fellowship of church.
Give us unity
in the midst of our diversity.
Give us hope
for the living of our days.
Bless our nation, Lord,
with homes and churches
which can make us strong in the Lord.
Help us understand
what it means to be
"One nation under God."
Forgive us, O Lord,
when we lose our grasp of holy things
and neglect the tie that binds us to all things.
Amen.

Chapter 12

THE WIND OF THE SPIRIT

Ezekiel 37:9-10; John 3:8; Acts 2:1-4

It is impossible to review the spiritual happenings of Christianity through the centuries without being strongly impressed with the miracle of God's Spirit. There is no way to explain the phenomenal growth and progress of Christianity apart from the involvement of God's powerful Spirit. It is amazing to see the Spirit at work in the quality of life and in the power of sheer goodness. The existence and the survival of the church are documented evidence of God's continuing miracle among us.

It is not always easy to define or to determine the operational procedures of God's Holy Spirit. There seem to be a certain freedom and autonomy about the Holy Spirit that often leave us baffled. We do not always understand the Spirit's unpredictable presence and His power to save in the most unlikely places.

Sometimes it seems that His Spirit ignores all our meticulous plans and prayers and chooses to visit us at unexpected times. How strange it is that all of a sudden we turn a corner in life and there is God, as big as life itself. Sometimes the dull and daily routine of life is suddenly interrupted by God's involvement. Sometimes church becomes the place where heaven comes down and glory fills our souls as God visits us with power and grace.

When He does visit us, however, we have a host of people who want to write a "how-to" book on it. Their titles read something like this: *How to Have a Revival in Five Easy Steps, How to Assure God's Presence, How to Work the Miracle of Church Renewal, How to Call Fire Down from Heaven,* and the titles go on. But let us not deal too harshly with these folks, because we buy their books. We buy their books in hopes that somebody somehow has learned the magic and the movement of God's Spirit.

The interesting thing about us is that we're always trying to find some way to predict and to define God. We want to analyze His activity and program His possibilities. In a sense, we are trying to manipulate and use God in some way if we can. It seems that we are endlessly trying to find some procedure that will guarantee His presence. We're forever trying to find the container into which we can put God and which will assure us that He will be there when we want Him.

But to our chagrin, we discover there is no such apparatus. Perhaps the greatest lesson we learn is there is no casual formula to explain the design of God's activity. Our finite minds cannot chart the course of God's mind. The work of God's Holy Spirit can never be reduced to simple-minded cliches. Our pious God-talk never means we have God under control.

There is an episode recorded in Acts in which

revival broke out in Samaria and Peter went down to share in that event. Miraculous things began to happen as God's Spirit was obviously at work. There was a magician in Samaria by the name of Simon. When he saw the phenomenal things that were happening, he asked to buy the Holy Spirit. He wanted to use its power in his own magic shows. Peter rebuked him for such a thought. He severely reprimanded him for misunderstanding the Holy Spirit. Peter made it quite clear that the miracles of God are not for sale. How do you bargain for the wind? How do you price that which you cannot define?

God is always bigger than our ability to understand. As someone has said, "If our reach cannot exceed our grasp, then what's a heaven for?" Our pilgrimage with God is one of faith. We see far more than we understand. If we walk in the light, however, the Holy Spirit will give us wisdom for the journey. He will show us as much as we need to know to be a pilgrim people.

The Bible gives us special insights at unique times concerning God's Holy Spirit. For example, ancient Hebrew people must have had some unusual insight into the Spirit of God. The Hebrew word for *spirit* is *ruach*, which means "wind," or "breath." The Hebrew mind, therefore, likened the Spirit of God to the wind that blows.

In the book of Ezekiel, that pastor/prophet among the lifeless exiles of Babylonian captivity was given a vision. He was shown a valley of dry bones and was commanded to preach to that pile of deadness. As he preached, flesh and skin began to cover the bones, but there was no life in them. Then Ezekiel was instructed by God to call upon the four winds. The winds of God blew upon those lifeless forms, and they became a mighty army. The reason why this vision from antiquity has any meaning whatsoever for us today is because that wind still blows. New life is a continuing possibility for us.

We get another glimpse of this wind in the gospel story. It was at night when Jesus encountered Nicodemus on the Mount of Olives. The wind must have been blowing up the valley, stirring the branches and leaves of the olive trees.

Jesus was speaking to Nicodemus about the work of God in the human soul. He talked to him about new birth and the possibilities of a new beginning. He must have talked about how God could take failure, emptiness, and sin in our lives and change us. He talked about fullness and vitality.

Nicodemus, however, could not understand. He was so caught up in a legal system of religion he could not grasp the meaning of grace. Although he was a master theologian and an accredited leader, he found these words of "new birth" quite beyond him.

Therefore, Jesus, searching for an illustration in the night, used what was already there. "Listen to the wind, Nicodemus. Listen to the wind. Do you hear its sound? The night is full of it. But where it has come from and where it is going, no one knows." In essence, Jesus was saying the Spirit of God is like that. It is invisible yet unmistakable. It is unpredictable yet full of power. "Stand in its path, Nicodemus. Turn your face toward it. Open your life to its influence, and it will do wonderful things for you. Just listen to the wind, that is, the wind of God."

Some years ago secular songwriter Bob Dylan wrote a song entitled "Blowin' in the Wind." In this song he asked several pertinent questions such as: "How many roads must a man walk down before you call him a man?" "How many times must the cannonballs fly before they're forever banned?" "How many years can some people exist before they're allowed to be free?" "How many times can a man turn his head, pretending he just doesn't see?" Dylan followed these and other questions with the refrain "The answer, my friend, is blowin' in the wind. The answer is blowin' in the wind."

Although this secular songwriter may have written more than he understood, there is a truth in this song. The answers to the pertinent questions of our day and the solutions to the complex dilemmas of our times are blowing in the wind. They are blowing in the wind of God's Spirit. Our need is to expose ourselves to this breath of God so that we may find the spiritual strength for our day.

Again, in the book of Acts we find evidence of this wind of God. It was the day of Pentecost when God's Spirit fell upon those orphan disciples. The writer could find no better way to describe that happening than to call it a mighty, rushing wind. It was a mighty wind as it blew upon those disciples and into the New Testament church, helping them to make a clearing for Christ in that wilderness of paganism.

That Pentecost event is a pivotal point in our understanding of God's involvement in His church. For one thing, we learn we are not nervously trying to protect a flickering flame. It is God's fire. That mighty, rushing wind is still blowing, and we do well to stand in its path. It can energize and equip us to be the people of God.

Furthermore, we read about this wind of God in relation to a man called Saul of Tarsus. Saul, whose name was later changed to Paul, was early Christianity's most obvious and unsuspecting convert. He was quite a dignitary in the ranks of Judaism. He had arrived at the top of the ecclesiastical ladder. But he had this thing about Christians, and he almost single-handedly took it upon himself to eliminate that so-called "new heresy."

We find him on his way to Damascus, armed with the credentials to destroy or to persecute any of those he found who were followers of the Christ. But on that road he ran headlong into the wind. So great was the impact of it that it left him physically impaired. What a difference it made in his soul! The difference between what he went to Damascus to do and what he left Damascus to say was a total turnaround. Paul began to listen to the wind, and it blew upon his life in such a way that his name has been eternally etched in the annals of Christendom.

Where are we today? How do we relate to this wind of God? To review these exciting episodes of God's power in the past still leaves us today with the nausea of our own inadequacies. We find ourselves wanting to ask, "Ezekiel, can the wind of God blow upon the dry bones of my own life?" "Peter, can the excitement of Pentecost be enacted again among the bored and passive spectators of our own congregations?" "Paul, can theologically sound and successfully proud people still encounter the wind of God on their individual Damascus roads?"

The answer to these questions and the good news of God in a nutshell is the word of Jesus to Nicodemus: "You can and you must be born again." The exciting news for all of us today is that new life is possible for every one of us. Pentecost with all of its power is not an impossibility for any church.

Yet some of us may be asking, "How can this be? What must we do?" Here we go, wanting another book that will tell us how to harness God. Perhaps it would be a two-year plan for spiritual resuscitation, or something similar. It is important to understand there is no magic formula. There are no "how-to-do-it" books.

Hopefully it doesn't make us feel spiritually insecure to realize there are no gimmicks or magic which can pull off a mighty revival. We really don't know how or when the mighty winds of God might blow. But we can know that if we want it badly enough it will happen. The wind of God's Spirit will blow upon us, and we will never be the same again. While there is no way to program the power of God into our lives, there are some helpful clues as we try to expose ourselves to the winds of His Spirit.

In the first place, we must learn to let it happen. We live in a world geared to make things happen. We often try to make things happen in church. We try our best to structure and program God's power into our lives and into our lifeless organizations. Often it does not work.

Jesus said, "The wind blows where it will." The truth implied here is there is freedom in the Spirit, and if we want it we must allow it to happen. Jesus asked the disciples to wait in Jerusalem until the Spirit came. Its coming would not be the result of their activity or ingenuity.

The prophet Isaiah said, "They that wait upon the Lord . . . shall mount up with wings as eagles; they shall run, and not be weary; and they shall walk, and not faint." The "waiting" referred to here is not idleness but creative anticipation. We wait, we pray, we prepare, and we listen for God's special timing.

The Spirit of God is a gift. Pentecost is a gift. Renewal is a gift. We must creatively anticipate its happening, and sooner than we might think, His wind will blow upon us.

In the second place, our exposure to the Holy Spirit depends upon being where God is. If His wind is to find us, if we want the vitality of His power, then we must involve ourselves in His kind of life. This means being in church and Christian worship and anywhere we are being spiritually equipped.

Yet it means much more. It means ministry out in the world where God is. It means being with the sick, with the lost, with the lonely, in the ghetto, and in the slums. It means stooping to wash the feet of a tired and dirty world and feeling the freshness of His wind upon our faces. It means working ourselves to exhaustion and then drying the sweat of our brow with the breezes of heaven. We cannot hide behind the shelters of apathy and indifference and expect God's wind to blow upon us. We must be out there where the wind is blowing. If we're not with God's people doing God's thing, then there's not much wind blowing where we are.

In the third place, our exposure to the Spirit of God depends upon our openness and receptivity to Him. One of the things that has always characterized Christianity's Pentecosts is *change*. Men and women were willing to change their attitudes, their conduct, and their whole lifestyles. The change was so radical for Saul of Tarsus he literally changed his name.

God's Spirit will not blow freely into the cracks and crevices of our own narrowness, bitterness, and prejudice. If we want God's wind to blow upon us, we must be open to new truths, new patterns, and new wineskins. Pentecost will never happen in our churches as long as we resist the winds of change.

Continuing conversion can happen for us as we

throw ourselves open to the wind of God. Being open and receptive allows the breath of heaven to blow a spiritual springtime upon the lifeless winter of our souls. Jesus told a scholarly Jew named Nicodemus that being open and receptive to God's wind was like a new birth, or a new beginning.

Does this mean that God is an elusive person? Does it mean His wind blows only on those occasions and on those people He chooses quite at random? No! No! It means we cannot always define His power. We cannot always put it into neat little packages and use it for our own little pieces of magic.

God's wind is always blowing, and on occasions when our hearts and souls are right, we can expose ourselves to the near side of God. That exposure both thrills us and disturbs us. It shakes the very roots of our personalities. We do not necessarily have to understand the wind; all we have to do is put up our sails and let it blow us into the center of God's will.

Many years ago there was a revival meeting going on in a little white frame church in the hills of western North Carolina. It was a most unimpressive place. An unconventional, rather awkward, and somewhat uneducated man was in the pulpit. There was nothing about the whole event that would appear to call fire down from heaven. But somehow the wind of God's Spirit began to blow upon that place, and a rebellious eighteen-year-old lad began to feel its breeze. It changed his life. It was a glorious thing that happened to that lad. I know because it was me.

I stood one night
    Holding fast the bench;
The Lord was calling;
    I would give not an inch.

My life was full
    Of sin and shame.
I did so much
    To dishonor His name.

In loneliness I stood
    As the altar did call;
The Holy Spirit's breeze
    On my soul did fall.

I left my seat
    And Satan, too;
I asked the Lord,
    "What shall I do?"

He said to me
    In a voice so sweet,
"Give me your all,
    From your head to your feet."

I said, "Dear Lord,
    To this request, I will."
And the sweet peace of God
    My heart did fill.

Sinner, if you are
Under the devil's spell
And want to escape
That awful place Hell,

Then put your trust
In the Lord above,
And let Him fill you
With His holy love.

REFLECTION

There was a sense of expectancy in the air as I sat meditating upon the possibility of renewal. Optimism prevailed as faith emerged from a prayerful dependency upon God.

I envisioned the wind of the spirit blowing upon the lifeless forms of a dead army. Just like in Ezekiel, bones which once had reflected the stench of an awful deadness were beginning to show signs of resurrection. The valley of dryness was coming alive with the showers of heavenly blessing. The desert was losing its ability to inflict death because the power of life had challenged its devastation. Flesh-and-blood people were now forming the nucleus of a mighty fellowship.

The word of the Lord was no longer falling on deaf ears. Soldiers of the cross were listening for their marching orders. People who had been walking in darkness were longing for the light. The thirst of a spiritual desert was calling for the living water. An ill-equipped army was putting on the armor of Christ.

It was an impressive miracle of grace to see the dawning of a new day. Hostility and resentment were taking a back seat to forgiveness and courtesy. People were so enamored with Jesus that His character was their character, and His thoughts were their thoughts. The prayer on everyone's lips was that His kingdom would come and His will would be done on earth as it is in heaven. What joy to see the excitement of folk who were beginning to give God the priority of their lives! Witnessing was on their agendas, and grace was in their hearts.

But then, quite legitimately, you ask, "How does one see such a resurgence of godly behavior on the human horizon?" It is through the eyes of faith that we see such divine possibilities. The essence of renewal is that we develop a sense of godly expectancy. The winds of God's spirit are blowing, and we prepare ourselves and invite others to experience their refreshing breeze.

The voice in the wilderness is a vision of a new hope which will not occur unless we look and see. To dream God's dream for a new day is the beginning of revival. Let us behold the glory of God's promised visitation.

PRAYER

Lord, our prayer is for renewal.
We are hungry for a fresh start.
We need the fires of our enthusiasm rekindled
by Your reviving grace.
We pray for a devotional life that is genuine
and a ministry that is effective.
Let the wind of Your spirit
blow into the cracks and crevices
of our neglected spirituality.
Give us a new day
with a new vision
of what we can do
and what we can be
in the context of Your call to discipleship.
We seek the truth
that will make us free.
We long for a love
that resembles You.
We ask for a witness
that focuses on You.
We knock on the door of opportunity
in order to be a servant people.
Hear our many prayers
without which, O Lord,
we would have no communion with You.
Amen.

Chapter 13

REASONS TO REJOICE

Acts 2:42-47; Philippians 4:4

Are you basically a happy person, or do you tend to be sad and somber? Are you happy in the Lord, or is God distant and dull to you? Are you happy in your church, or is religion a meaningless routine?

Because God is a "happiness" God, it is important for you and me to be happy. It is essential that our happiness be grounded in God since we are created in His image.

The Bible is a "happiness" book. Its truths point to the path of happiness. It invites us to express our happiness as we praise the Lord in song, in dance, and with musical instruments.

The church is a "happiness" people. It provides a place and a program where our joy can be contagious. Its worship gives us a reason to rejoice.

But where are we today? Does our public praise reveal our inner happiness? I remember a little chorus we sang as youngsters. Some of the words go like this:

If you're happy and you know it,
    say "Amen."
If you're happy and you know it,

say "Amen."
If you're happy and you know it,
    then your face will surely show it.
If you're happy and you know it,
    say "Amen."

If you're happy and you know it,
    clap your hands.
If you're happy and you know it,
    clap your hands.
If you're happy and you know it,
    then your face will surely show it.
If you're happy and you know it
    clap your hands.

Some may think that's a little shallow for our sophisticated minds. But wouldn't it make us all feel good to let a little happiness out by singing like children again? I know the song is a bit simplistic, but maybe the simple is what we need. Perhaps the complicated and the technical have hindered our happiness in the Lord.

Someone has said, "The church suffers today from a lack of old-fashioned, simple-hearted, overflowing Christian joy. We have plenty of knowledge, enthusiasm, and denominational zeal, but the Lord's happiness has left us. Churches that started out in the fires of revival are now living only in the smoke. We assemble on the Lord's Day as though to mourn a defeat rather than to celebrate a victory."

When we look at the New Testament church, we see those early Christians eating their meat with gladness and singleness of heart, praising God. We hear Paul shouting from his prison cell, "Rejoice in the Lord always, and again I say, rejoice!" The dominant note of that post-Pentecost church, even in the face of severe persecution, was one of triumphant joy. Let us learn from them why we have many reasons to rejoice.

For one thing, our most basic reason to rejoice is found in Jesus Christ, the King of joy. The New Testament, which begins with an angel chorus and ends with rejoicing around the throne of God, reminds us that the good news centers in Jesus Christ, the Son of God. Those early Christians not only heard, but they experienced the good news of Jesus. They found in Him the basis of their happiness. The Holy Spirit invaded their lives and left them with the fruit of joy, even as Jesus had promised.

During His earthly ministry, one of Jesus' most characteristic greetings was "Be of good cheer." It was this spiritual optimism that made disciples out of ordinary men and women. It brought health and courage to all who trusted Him.

On one occasion when Jesus healed a paralytic man, He said, "Be of good cheer; your sins are forgiven you." Jesus was offering the cheer of forgiveness, without which there can be no happiness. The thrust of this miracle is seen in the fact that Jesus associated healing with forgiveness.

The truth here is that we have neither health nor

happiness until the sin problem is faced. When conscience goes in one direction and conduct in another, the springs of happiness dry up. We are healthiest and happiest when the physical, spiritual, and mental aspects of our being are in harmony with one another.

Will Rogers tells a story about a hardworking druggist. He was asked one day if he ever went out and really lived it up. The druggist said, "No, I don't. But I sell a lot of headache medicine to those who do."

Sin is the culprit that robs us of both health and happiness. Jesus was saying something we all need to hear when He said, "Be of good cheer; your sins are forgiven." He offers us the good cheer of forgiveness.

He also offers us the good cheer of His presence. One night as the disciples were struggling with their boat on the windy sea, Jesus walked out to them. At first they were startled, but Jesus said, "Be of good cheer! It is I; do not be afraid." The disciples had learned to lose their anxiety in the presence of Jesus.

Tension, frustration, and fear are some of the most common enemies of happiness. They can paralyze our potential for joy and render us useless in His kingdom. Even today He comes offering us the cheer and the joy of His presence. Do you hear His voice? He tells us we can be happy pilgrims.

Near the end of His ministry, Jesus gave His disciples a cheer of victory. He warned them of the tribulation that lay ahead. He told them that the world would not deal kindly with them. But He said with great assurance, "Be of good cheer, for I have overcome the world."

One of the main reasons the early Christians could rejoice was because their focus was on Jesus. For this reason they could break bread together with gladness and singleness of heart. The same crucified and risen Christ invites us to open the door and sup with Him and He with us. Because He invites us to a feast and not a funeral, we have a reason to rejoice.

Another strong reason we have to rejoice is in the assurance of our salvation. Luke's gospel tells us of a time when Jesus sent out seventy folk to witness in His name. When they returned, they were excited and rejoiced in the fact that even the demons were subject to them.

Jesus responded to their excitement in this way. He said, "Do not rejoice . . . that the spirits are subject to you, but rather rejoice because your names are written in heaven." Jesus was focusing on a deeper reason to rejoice. Jesus did not discount the joy of their seeing marvelous things happen. He did not want them to get so excited over what they had done they would forget what had been done for them.

Our deepest joy does not come from what we can do, but from what has been done for us. As Wallace Hamilton has said, "No one writes his or her own name in heaven any more than one signs his or her own birth certificate." We have a reason to rejoice as we reflect upon who we are by the grace of God.

From this perspective, God has given each of us a lot of attention.

Jesus said in John 10, "My sheep listen to my voice; I know them and they follow me. I give them eternal life and they shall never perish. No one can snatch them out of my hand."

Paul reflects the same thought to the Philippian Christians when he wrote, "He who began a good work in you will carry it on to completion until the day of Christ Jesus."

The last sentence of the letter of Jude says, "To Him who is able to keep you from falling and to present you before His glorious presence without fault and with great joy . . . be glory, majesty, power and authority, through Jesus Christ our Lord, before all ages, now and forevermore!" Because of the sense of security we have in Christ Jesus, we have a strong reason to rejoice.

A third reason we have to rejoice is *people*. Of course, people can cause us much grief. They can cut us, hurt us, and maliciously malign us. People can be our greatest source of frustration, confusion, and downright despair. You may feel if it were not for certain folk, your life would be free of many of its headaches. It is true. The devil uses people to launch his hard attacks against us.

On the other hand, however, God seeks to offset the satanic snare of those who would do us in with a corps of caring folk who would lift us up. Although the capacity for hate and harm is prevalent all around us, there is also a dimension of love. Where would we be today were it not for the influence of godly parents? What about the encouragement we receive from a loving church family? God has prepared a person or a combination of persons who bring us relief amid the trials and tribulations of life.

Not only can we rejoice in the fact that people give us help and hope, but we can also rejoice in the fact that we can help them as well. Paul had tender words for his Christian friends at Philippi. He referred to them as "my brethren," "my joy," "my crown," and "my dearly beloved." Paul rejoiced in the fact that he had those dear people toward whom he could fulfill his calling and ministry.

Here, then, is a truth worth learning. Happiness is a by-product of self-forgetting devotion. When we center upon ourselves, we quickly become the kind of self we do not enjoy living with. Happy people are not asking "What do I want?" but "What is wanted of me?"

A famous medical doctor tells that unhappy people with health problems often ask him, "Is life worth living?" His common reply is, "It all depends on the liver." Happy people are people with a mission, a calling, and a task.

John Balderson has written a play about a man who died and opened his eyes in the next world. He saw beauty and luxury beyond description. His every wish was granted. Nothing was withheld, and everything was done for him.

After a while he grew restless and impatient. He

longed for something to do. He wanted something to create and some challenge to accept. He wanted something to break his idle monotony.

One day he asked the attendant for something to do. He wanted some task that would stretch his capabilities. The attendant said he was sorry, but that wish could not be granted. At that the man lost his temper in rage and said, "In that case, I don't wish to be here. I would rather be in hell!" whereupon the attendant replied, "And where do you think you are, sir?"

It is hell to be alive and not have a reason to live. Not having a reason to live is tantamount to losing our reason to rejoice. There is no greater source of happiness than the fact that we have a calling to care for one another. Indeed, we can find service to others a legitimate reason to rejoice.

Of course, there are many other reasons to rejoice. Everyone has his or her own reasons to rejoice. The important thing is that we rejoice in the Lord. The big truth we need to consider is that rejoicing seems to be a scriptural command. Paul said, "Rejoice in the Lord always, and again I say, rejoice!"

There is an epitaph which reads, "Died--age 30; buried--age 60." Too many people have an emotional and spiritual death early, but their bodies do not demise until much later. If you are losing your zest for living, then allow Jesus, the King of joy, to offer you many reasons to rejoice again.

REFLECTION

It's a wonderful thing to be alive, to be able to breathe, to see, to smell, to taste, and to touch. These things which we often take for granted are so vital to the meaning of life. God in His creative grace has chosen to share a bit of His existence with us, and we call it "life." He has given this energy of existence to all living things, and we are blessed by it.

The sights and sounds of life explode before us, and we are often unaware of their presence. The laughter of children, the buzz of bees, chirping birds, trees, flowers, friendship, and worship are just some of the things that give a sense of awe and celebration to being alive.

Sometimes the crises of life pungently bring to our attention those simple aspects of our daily routines which have a marvelous capacity for our nurture. Often in our search for the profound we miss the profundity of the simple. In our haste to show up at the important events of life, we miss a thousand opportunities to allow little things to prepare us for big things.

I could ramble on and on about this thought because a prolonged illness gave me a view I never took enough time to see before. How rapidly I was running through life searching for the significant when daily I was missing some of life's most profound pictures!

Life has its own candid camera as well as its

serious productions. My dear church friends have starred in many years of visual aids and have been a wonderfully congenial cast. It's a video victory when we have eyes to see and can really see. It's an audio miracle to have ears to hear and really hear.

PRAYER

Thank You, Lord, for the joy of life.
Thank You
for allowing us to share human existence.
We celebrate Who You are
and who we are
when You intersect our lives.
You give us many reasons to rejoice.
We rejoice in Your creative power.
Your love calls forth our praise.
We stand in awe of Your beauty.
We are glad
when we are in the house of the Lord.
We sing
because we are happy.

*We pray
because we are encouraged to hope.
We study Your Word.
We meditate upon Your goodness.
We find joy in our fellowship with You
and with those who love You.
Forgive our sad and somber ways.
Forgive the lifeless monotony of our daily routines
and restore unto us the joy of our salvation.
May honor, glory, and power be with us
now and forevermore.
Amen.*

EPILOGUE

Everyone loves a story with a happy ending. We like our heroes to go riding off into the sunset to live happily ever after. We like happy endings because we want everything to turn out good in the end for people we like and for ourselves.

Life, however, does not always give us happy endings. Some things in the story of our lives end up in disarray. There are chapters in the sequences of events that shape our lives which have sad conclusions. Of course, life as we try to put it together will have an assortment of endings. When we try to write the pages of our personal history all by ourselves, we face a barrage of unpredictable conclusions.

Only in Christ can we fully know the meaning of happy endings. Only He who is the author and finisher of our faith can write the scripts for our lives with positive benedictions. In Him, the sins which produce sadness are conquered by His chastising grace. In Him, the fear that produces failure is absorbed in the courage of commitment. In Him, the prospects for bitterness and resentment are relieved amid His encouragement to forgive. In Christ Jesus, the sad-ending chapters of our lives can enhance the beauty of our being because He works for our good in everything if we love Him and are called according to His purpose.

The fact that we shall live again in God's eternal glory means that life's episodes with unhappy endings need not lead us to despair. Our ultimate happiness is not attached to the perishable treasures of this life, but to the power and the glory of the Lord forever and ever. In Him, we are constantly reminded that one day we shall live happily ever after.

In the meantime, let us add fullness to one another's lives. The fellowship of love enables us to use our dippers and buckets wisely. Happiness is the by-product of putting more in than we take out of each other's buckets. A full bucket makes for a happy ending.